The Primary Teacher's Handbook

Lyn Overall and Margaret Sangster

continuum
LONDON • NEW YORK

Continuum

The Tower Building
11 York Road
London SE1 7NX

15 East 26th Street
New York
NY 10010

www.continuumbooks.com

First published 2003
Reprinted 2004

British Library Cataloguing-in-Publication Data
A catalogue record for this book is available from the British Library.

ISBN: 0–8264–5677–4 (hardback) 0–8264–5678–2 (paperback)

Typeset by C.K.M. Typesetting, Salisbury, Wiltshire
Printed and bound in Great Britain by MPG Books Ltd, Bodmin, Cornwall

Contents

List of headwords   vii

Introduction   1

Part One: The self-evaluation process   5

Part Two: A–Z of effective teaching strategies   19

List of headwords

Able children 21
Active learning 22
Assessment (see Baseline assessment, Feedback, Formative assessment,
    Self-assessment by pupils, Summative assessment) 26
Baseline assessment 26
Behaviour 27
Bullying 27
Challenge (see Expectations about pupils' learning) 30
Child development 30
Child protection 31
Code of Practice 35
Communicating clearly 39
Communication about learning 41
Communication with parents 44
Competition 46
Completed work 47
Connexions 49
Consolidation 49
Continuing professional development (CPD) 50
Culture 52
Curriculum 54
Demonstration by the teacher 58
Differentiation 61
Discipline 63
Displays 67
Early learning goals 68
Emotional development 70
English as an additional language 71
Equal opportunities 73
Ethnicity 76
Evaluating lessons (assessing the meeting of learning objectives) 77
Expectations about pupils' learning (challenge) 79
Expectations of pupils' behaviour (see Discipline) 81
Explaining 81
Feedback 82
Formative assessment (monitoring pupils' learning) 84
Gender 86
Group work 88
Harassment (see Bullying) 90
Homework 90
ICT (Information and Communication Technology) 92

Inclusion   94
Independent learning   97
Instruction   99
Intellectual development   101
Intervention   103
Learning objectives   105
Learning styles   107
Lesson plan structure   109
Level descriptions   112
Linguistic development   113
Listening and responding to pupils   115
Long-term planning   117
Marking   119
Medium-term planning   121
Misconceptions and remedies   123
Monitoring pupils' learning (see Formative assessment)   125
More able children (see Able children)   125
Motivation   125
Out-of-school learning opportunities   127
Pace   129
Parents   131
Physical development   132
Play and structured learning   134
Problem solving   136
Purposeful working atmosphere   138
Questioning   139
Recording individual progress   141
Relationships with pupils   143
Research and its uses   145
Resources   148
Rewards   150
Safety   152
Self-assessment by pupils   154
Skills and strategies   156
Social development   157
Special Educational Needs   159
Standardized tests   167
Subject knowledge   168
Summative assessment   170
Target setting   171
Teachers' employment and conditions   173
Teaching in teams   175
Thinking skills (including cognitive acceleration)   177
Time management   179
Timing within lessons   181
Transitions   182
Values and ethos   184
Whole class teaching   186
Working with other adults   188

Introduction

This book is about working on becoming a more effective teacher through a process of evaluation and action.

> *Outstanding teachers continuously set and meet ambitious targets for themselves and their pupils. They refer regularly to visible, quantifiable and tangible measures; and they focus on whether they and the school are making a difference and adding value to pupils.*
>
> (Hay McBer, 2000, 1.3.9)

When effective teachers talk about how they work it is hard for them to express the complexity of decision making which occurs from minute to minute in managing a class. Success is a mixture of hard work, knowledge, personality, professional commitment and the implementation of a range of teaching skills. Professional knowledge and teaching skills are acquired and refined over many years. This book offers an analytical reflection on teaching strategies and a model for implementation of those strategies. From our experience of observing teachers and students at work, we feel that the self-evaluation process is one of the most effective ways to develop teaching skills.

Teaching is one of those professions in which it is difficult to feel you know enough to cope with everything that comes your way. There always appear to be new situations to deal with; a pupil who tests all your current strategies and patience; a new initiative to introduce; a new technology to assimilate. The feeling of 'I need to know more' never goes away throughout your career. In our ever-changing society, it would not be too extreme to say that we have come to accept an element of continuous development in most professional work.

As a student in training the learning curve is steep and initially driven by survival! Gradually the focus moves away from yourself to questions about pupils' learning and the effectiveness of the strategies that you are using. Students who learn most rapidly are those who reflect on their own development and take action to improve their teaching. You may identify areas which need development and set your own targets on which to work. The class teacher and the mentor will help you with this. This book is written to support that target setting.

In March 2001 a new initiative 'Teaching and Learning' (DfES, 2001) was launched by the government to enhance teachers' continuing professional development. There is an expectation that teachers will continue to develop their skills and qualifications and an indication that teachers will, in future, track their own professional development in a profile document. This already happens with newly qualified teachers (TTA, 1998). As a teacher you may choose to further develop your teaching strategies and will find the contents of this book a useful starting point.

Teachers are not the only adults who work with children in school. Often co-workers, for example Nursery Nurses and Classroom Assistants, are placed in charge of a group or work with individual pupils. They are faced with similar situations to the class teacher. The strategies employed to deal with these situations will, on many occasions, be the same as those used by the teacher. Within these pages there are suggestions which will support the management of groups and individuals.

Within the book there is information on aspects of teaching, suggested teaching strategies and reference as to where you can obtain further information on topics. Many entries are mapped to official documentation about teacher training in England (DfEE/TTA, 2002).

Although the entries can be used purely as reference material, their main contribution will be as a practical support to developing teaching strategies in the classroom. Part One outlines how the teaching strategies can be developed as part of the process of self-evaluation. This is followed in Part Two by an A–Z of topics which promote the development of effective teaching strategies. Each entry has a first section to help you think about what is involved in the topic. Links are then made with other relevant topics in the book. This is followed by bullet pointed strategies for you to select as targets. An additional section offers further discussion on each topic. There are also some suggestions for further reading.

References

Department for Education and Skills (DfES) (2001) *Teaching and Learning*, London: DfES.

Department for Education and Skills/Teacher Training Agency (DfES/TTA) (2002) *Qualifying to Teach, Professional Standards for Qualified Teacher Status and Requirements for Initial Teacher Training*, London: TTA, publication no. TPU 0803/02-02 (weblink www.canteach.gov.uk).

Hay McBer (2000) *Research into Teacher Effectiveness: A Model of Teacher Effectiveness*, Department for Education and Employment (weblink www.dfes.gov.uk/teachingreforms/leadership/mcber/).

Teacher Training Agency (TTA) (1998) *Career Entry Profile for Newly Qualified Teachers*, London: TTA.

Part One

The self-evaluation process

The self-evaluation process

We have observed over a period of years that the student teachers and teachers who make best use of the evaluation process make good progress in their effectiveness in the classroom. They work on how to manage a classroom and how to provide an effective learning environment for their pupils. The process they use is similar to the assessment process that takes place with pupils in class. It is accepted that assessment is a part of ensuring good pupil progress. Teachers look at pupils' work and comment on their progress against set criteria. This collection and evaluation of data are two steps in the assessment process. A third step is to act upon the results by planning an appropriate next step to take with the pupils. This process is known as formative assessment. It is an essential stage in the teaching cycle. It is not enough to say, 'I have planned this, I have taught this and that's my job done'.

Effective teachers respond to the needs of the pupils in their class. They adapt and adjust work so that it builds on pupils' current knowledge. When discovering misconceptions, effective teachers backtrack and re-teach, so that pupils have correct understanding. Assessment allows teachers to recognize where pupils are in their learning and to respond accurately to pupils' needs. This can be described as a *cycle of teaching* which *spirals* forward as assessment informs the next planning.

- teaching – assessing (recording) – planning – teaching – assessing –

In this book we are suggesting that you apply a parallel cycle of self-evaluation and target-setting to your own teaching skills. By *closing the loop* on your own learning by assessing your needs and taking action, you can generate a model that carries the development of your teaching skills forward. You, or a mentor you are working with, identify a target for improvement. You then decide on a strategy to deal with the situation and try it out. Then, most important of all, you then need to assess whether your strategy was effective and can be used again, or whether you must try another. It is easy to see how this will enable you to build a repertoire of successful strategies for use in your work.

The process of self-evaluation

The process of self-evaluation has several steps. These lead you through the decision making that is required to solve a problem, meet a challenge or make a minor adjustment to your teaching. The steps are:

1. Identify the cause for your concern – name the issue.
2. Consider the available strategies.
3. Select a strategy.
4. Try it out.
5. Did it work?
6. If yes – keep it in the repertoire.
7. If no – select another strategy and try again.
8. Start again at 1 on the next strategy.

1. Identify the cause for your concern – name the issue

If something is not going well in the classroom you will want to make improvements. If it is a problem, first you have to identify it – naming what you think it is. For example, you note that in your lesson:

> some pupils are getting bored;
> there is some poor behaviour;
> some able children are disengaging from work and are under-performing.

This combination might have several causes but after some thought about this, you decide that your planning and task for the lesson are fine, the problem is that the pace is slow. The slow pace is boring some pupils, giving rise to poor behaviour and less than satisfactory work. It could have been a combination of problems, but this time you decide it is one problem that gives rise to several 'symptoms' that you want to improve.

In this book, if you are sure you know what is causing the problem you can look up the cause directly. Sometimes you may have to read several sections and follow the links before you find comments that match the situation you are considering.

As the process of identifying the cause to be addressed and naming the issue may take some working out, it is often helpful to discuss the situation with an experienced teacher. They can often pinpoint the main cause and help you to consider appropriate strategies. If you are a student teacher this consultation procedure will be part of your training.

2. Consider the available strategies

Once you have identified the area in which you are working, you need to select a strategy. Some possible strategies are offered under each heading. You might feel that one or several of these are appropriate. Reading the commentary and reflecting on the issue could help you to formulate a strategy of your own.

3. Select a strategy

Select the strategy which you think will be most effective in your situation. You may wish to select more than one strategy and trial them simultaneously. Trying out a strategy might involve refining that strategy until it is effective. It might be that you set three targets to work at simultaneously. These may or may not be linked. A linked example would be that you have a child whose behaviour you wish to change and you have three strategies that you are going to try out. In the following example there are three strategies for dealing with a child who can be disruptive:

(i) You are going to ignore interruption during the whole class 'carpet' session and deal with behaviour at the end.

(ii) You are going to ensure that the child starts on the task by sharing the first few minutes with him/her.

(iii) You are always going to finish any conversation with the child with a statement of praise about one positive aspect of his/her work or behaviour.

4. Try it out

Having decided what you are going to do, try it. You may decide to trial your chosen strategy over one or more days.

5. Did it work?

It is important to evaluate the effectiveness of what you chose to do. Sometimes the strategy you've chosen will take time to have an effect. Sometimes it becomes clear quite quickly that the strategy is not the right one for the context. Returning to ask whether it worked or not is part of the conscious process of permanently adopting the strategy or throwing it out.

6. If yes – keep it in the repertoire

If the strategy worked then give yourself a pat on the back and make sure you keep using it for as long as it is appropriate.

7. If no – select another strategy and try again

Not everything is going to work first time. It is worth talking to someone about the situation if the strategy does not work. He/she might have a different view on the cause and can help you think through the possible solutions. It might be that you have selected an appropriate strategy, but it is going to take time to work. Some children can be resistant for the whole year! You might, now you have thought and observed more about the situation, decide that a different strategy is more appropriate.

8. On to the next strategy

If you have been successful you will be ready to work on another problem, challenge, or minor adjustment in your teaching, so move on to your next target. If success has eluded you, have a rethink and persevere with the same strategy or select a new one. It is important to sustain the momentum and make the evaluative process part of your normal practice.

A format to support the self-evaluation process

Figure 1 shows a suggested format that allows for three 'visits' to the self-evaluation process. It is followed by two examples of how it can be used in conjunction with this book. Example 1 is drawn from a need identified by a student from his/her classroom experience. Example 2 is from a teacher seeking to improve an aspect of his/her work.

Self-evaluation of teaching strategies	
The aspect of teaching or learning I wish to improve	
Strategy to try	Evaluation
	Success/try another strategy
The aspect of teaching or learning I wish to improve	
Strategy to try	Evaluation
	Success/try another strategy
The aspect of teaching or learning I wish to improve:	
Strategy to try	Evaluation
	Success/try another strategy

Figure 1 Format to support the self-evaluation process

EXAMPLE 1: MARIE'S TRANSITIONS

Marie, a student teacher, realizes that she is having difficulty moving the class from one place to another. One of the times is when they all finish one activity and have to move to the next, such as moving from the whole class teaching on the carpet to group activities at the tables. The children are noisy, start to wander round the class, some finding other things to do. She usually ends up raising her voice, stopping everyone and telling them off. Particularly difficult is the time when children finish their work at different times. These periods of time are known as 'transitions'.

Having identified where the problem lies she looks in the A–Z section at *Transitions*. Here she finds that there are several types of transitions and several possible causes for them not going smoothly. At this point she needs to select what she is going to work on first. Is it going to be: clearer instructions; a different strategy for getting children to move from one place to another; or a change in the work set? She may wish to take on more than one strategy. The important point is for Marie to identify what is causing the problem. She may be able to discuss this with her class teacher who has been observing her teaching.

Having selected the strategy to try out, Marie then needs to write it on the form.

Self-evaluation of teaching strategies

The aspect of teaching or learning I wish to improve

Transitions

Strategy to try	Evaluation
Clearer end of task instructions. *Sending groups one at a time from carpet to tables.*	
	Success/try another strategy

At this stage only 'The aspect of teaching or learning I wish to improve' and the 'Strategy to try' sections are completed. At the end of the day Marie returns to the form to do her evaluation and consider her next target.

Self-evaluation of teaching strategies

The aspect of teaching or learning I wish to improve

Transitions

Strategy to try	**Evaluation**
Clearer end of task instructions.	*I still need to work on this.*
Sending groups one at a time from carpet to tables.	*This was much better, I shall keep this.*
	Success/try another strategy

The aspect of teaching or learning I wish to improve.

Continue with transitions.

Strategy to try	**Evaluation**
Clearer end of task instructions with sitting or lining up place included.	
	Success/try another strategy

From the way Marie fills in the evaluation we can see she has had some partial success. She wishes to change one of her strategies slightly and focus again on it. She will maintain the successful strategy of sending them off to work, a group at a time.

EXAMPLE 2: PETER'S MARKING STRATEGIES

Peter, a teacher in his second year of teaching, has noticed that many of his Year 5 class pay little attention to the marks he gives for maths and English. Currently he operates a system where children receive a mark out of 10 for each piece of work. These he collects in a record book and averages out for the half-term. He occasionally writes a brief phrase such as 'good work', 'satisfactory' or 'see me' on the pupils' books. He would like his pupils to show more concern about errors and improving their performance.

Self-evaluation of teaching strategies

The aspect of teaching or learning I wish to improve

Pupil engagement in addressing errors.

Strategy to try	Evaluation
Time slot to discuss errors with peers and whole class.	
	Success/try another strategy

On reflection and having read the sections in this book on marking and feedback, he feels he has two choices: to instigate a more competitive environment; or to involve the pupils in reviewing and evaluating their own work. He is not sure whether these two strategies are mutually exclusive, but opts to try the second strategy.

Peter decides to begin the next maths lesson with pupils discussing with each other any mistakes they had made. He is aware he might have to pair some children who had 10 out of 10 with those who had made many mistakes.

Peter found that the discussion was useful because the pupils fed back to him that they were now more comfortable with the maths. This was a gain, but the start of the session was very ragged and much session time was taken up. Peter therefore decided to adjust his strategy to make it more structured. He was not sure whether this would increase or decrease pupil understanding, but was prepared to seek further feedback from pupils.

Self-evaluation of teaching strategies

The aspect of teaching or learning I wish to improve

Pupil engagement in addressing errors

Strategy to try	Evaluation
Time slot to discuss errors with peers and whole class.	*Peer discussion took longer than expected, but pupils were clearer about where they had gone wrong.*
	Whole class discussion made it even longer and pupils not forthcoming about mistakes.
	Success/try another strategy

The aspect of teaching or learning I wish to improve		
Continue with pupil engagement in addressing errors, but reduce time involved.		

Strategy to try	Evaluation
I will select most common mistake to discuss with whole class to start with,	
then,	**Success/try another strategy**
5 minute time limit on peer discussion if needed.	

> Whilst the strategy Peter tried has led to more engagement by the pupils he has now gone on to question how meaningful giving marks out of 10 are and how constructive his comments are to the pupils. He has begun to examine further his assessment and feedback strategies.

Further uses of evaluation strategies and target setting in teaching

In Part Two, the entries which are most directly about teaching, include suggested strategies which are written in the present tense, in an instructional form. This is for use when carrying out the strategy in the classroom, for example, 'Allow 10 minutes for a plenary', 'Check the clock every 10 minutes to see if I am on schedule'. By changing the form to a question it can also be used as a check when planning. For example, 'Have I allowed time for a plenary?'. When evaluating the success of your strategy you will move into question mode again, for example, 'Did I allow time for the plenary?, Did I check the clock?'.

Self-evaluation is a powerful process. Here we are recommending that you use it on your teaching skills. The same procedure can also be used in evaluating the effectiveness of a lesson. Did the lesson meet the objective? If yes, well done and move on. If no, then what shall I change next time?

It is also useful to use the process with individual pupils. For example, if you have a shy child you can consider what strategy you can use to encourage him/her to join in group discussion. At the end of the week you can assess whether your strategy has been effective. This could be recorded in the pupils' ongoing profiles. As well as being a proactive way of working with children, it also helps you to be consistent in your responses, which sends clear messages about behaviour to the children in your class.

International perspectives

This book is mostly about generic teaching skills. The strategies suggested will apply to many contexts. In countries where students training to be teachers are required to meet criteria or competencies or professional standards, entries can be 'mapped' against these. These could be integrated into the target-setting and recorded in the official profile. In England, to qualify to teach, statutory requirements have to be met (DfES/TTA, 2002). Where they apply we have mapped entries against these requirements. Some of the information-giving entries are about primary education in England, while some are of general application.

A note on terminology

Words mean different things in different countries. This book uses English terms. We write about our school-age learners as children, pupils or students. In the USA and Canada, learners of all ages are students. In the USA, Canada and in some South American countries, grades equate to chronological age but progression to the next grade is based on competence. In the rest of the world, children are usually grouped by chronological age and progress with advancing age. In England, most children enter schooling before they are 5, some start nursery education when they are 3. The 5-year-olds go into a reception class. At 6 they progress to a Year 1 class, which normally equates to Grade 1 in most of the USA, and to Primary 2 in Scotland. In the UK, children are in primary school until the age of 11. These are known as elementary schools in Canada and the USA. Eleven to 18-year-olds in the UK go to secondary school, in North America, Australia and New Zealand these students attend high school.

In the UK education system, central government determines much of the structure and provision for education. For example, in England there is a National Curriculum with Key Stage tests at 7, 11 and 14. There are also national qualifications, usually by public examination, at end stages of secondary education. There is also a national inspection system. Wales, Scotland and Northern Ireland have their own systems.

In England, whilst funding is increasingly channelled directly into schools, local government in the form of local education authorities (LEAs) also allocate funds from local and central taxation. This has reduced the role of the local authority education department. Contrast this with North America, where diversity is considerable as education is a district and state responsibility. Some states have an outline curriculum and take part in some national examinations for older students, but it is not possible to generalize.

Terminology varies in internal matters too. For example, in English schools the senior manager is usually known as the head teacher, whilst in North America, the senior manager in school is known as the school principal. In the UK, the free time between lessons is known as breaks; whilst it is called recess in North America. School work in the UK is marked; in the USA it is graded.

References

Department for Education and Skills/Teacher Training Agency (DfES/TTA) (2002) *Qualifying to Teach Professional Standards for Qualified Teacher Status and Requirements for Initial Teacher Training*, London: TTA, publication no. 0803/02-02 (weblink www.canteach.gov.uk).

Part Two

A–Z of effective teaching strategies

Able children

Often able children are talented in many aspects of school work. Occasionally a child has a talent in one specific area such as music, art or mathematics. Able children's cycle of learning has a different balance. Often there is a quick uptake of new learning, with the child making links to his/her prior experience. They need only a short consolidation or practice period, and enjoy applying the learning to new and challenging situations. Problem solving is a good example of one way of meeting able children's needs.

Sometimes able children become withdrawn. Sometimes they get impatient with slower children and prefer to work on their own. As a teacher you have to find the balance between developing all aspects of the child, including working with others. You need to create opportunities which let the child stretch his/her abilities.

Some children are educationally advanced because they are more mature or, they have received rich educational experiences at home, or have been coached in a subject. It is the teacher's task to work out what each child is capable of and provide a suitably challenging curriculum.

Links

Differentiation
Expectations about pupils' learning
Group work
Problem solving

Strategies

- Increase an able student's decision-making opportunities.
- Lessen practice time and increase time spent on application of knowledge.
- Try presenting work initially as a problem.
- Adjust the group task so it is more challenging for the able child.
- Try to find times when able children work with you and with other able children.

Development

Much has been written about able children and gifted children. It is recognized that children can be talented at different things. Gardner

(1983) theorizes that multiple intelligences exist and the brain develops with strengths in a possible seven areas, such as spatial intelligence, music intelligence and numerical intelligence. It is generally recognized that Intelligence Quotient (IQ) tests are a rather general way of measuring ability and it is more effective to deal with specific abilities. This is not easy when teaching classes of 30 children. When trying to establish what able children know, it appears they can do all the things you ask of them within the normal range of the curriculum for your year group. It is probable that they can do half the work before you teach them so it is understandable that they get bored. It is vital that they engage in new learning. This may mean that you have to cater for their needs on an individual basis.

Alongside the academic needs of the able child, the teacher needs to ensure that social development and good working practices are addressed. It is very easy to isolate able children. They get impatient when working with children who think at a slower speed to them. They get fed up acting as a surrogate teacher. Other children can treat them as 'different' and find them threatening. They can easily get used to working on their own and some find it slow and tedious to articulate their thinking. A variety of approaches and experiences need to be utilized, appropriate to the expected outcomes of the task. Muijs and Reynolds (2001) offer a good account of the needs and organization of gifted children in the classroom.

Further reading

Gardner, H. (1983) *Frames of Mind: A Theory of Multiple Intelligences,* London: Heinemann.

Muijs, D. and Reynolds, D. (2001) *Effective Teaching: Evidence and Practice,* London: Paul Chapman.

TTA Standards

3.2.4, 3.3.4.

Active learning

How can we put children in a position to control their own learning? To be active learners they need to be able to:

forecast how well they will do on various tasks;

know what they already understand about the tasks;
know what aspects of the tasks they can do.

Active learners can transfer what they know to new tasks. In a modern society active learning is important because individuals will need to be able to do new things as new challenges arise. Our responsibility is to enable children to reflect on and improve their own abilities to learn. There are three important ideas that underpin active learning: formative assessment; thorough teaching; and teaching children how to learn.

Open formative assessment   Children come to our schools knowing many things. We have to know and use what each of them understands about what they are learning. This has implications for assessment. In the model of active learning it is not sufficient to test at end points. Assessment has to be a continuous monitoring of knowledge and understanding. Constructive and supportive feedback helps to make explicit to the individual what he/she knows and what still has to be learned. It is a way of modelling the process of reflective learning.

Teach less, more thoroughly   Coverage of the curriculum is important but we don't have to teach everything all at once. Trying to cover everything means that much of what is taught is without depth. Knowledge, concepts and skills can be carefully managed to ensure coverage during the school years. However, this is not to deny the importance of completeness in any subject. Rather it suggests that an in-depth understanding of subject concepts and factual knowledge is more important that superficial coverage of the whole discipline. You'll know that parts of the subjects you teach can be hard to grasp. Your job is to make learning, 'the hard to grasp bit', possible. You'll do this by giving an overview, 'This is what we are learning'. Breaking the learning into small steps and relating these back to what children are learning. It helps to use a great many examples about one concept. It is important that the children find the learning as easy as possible. As some children are resistant to challenge, it is important to avoid indicating that what they are doing is hard to learn. You will want to be encouraging, 'You are working hard', whilst they are learning. You will want to celebrate success by telling them, 'You're clever at this now'. End-point assessment should test children's deep understanding rather than their surface knowledge. This also ensures public accountability.

Taking time to ensure that children's factual knowledge is accurate and secure is very important. To do this your own understanding of factual knowledge and the concepts of the subjects you teach and their disciplines (ways of working and thinking) are crucial. Of equal importance is your knowledge about how children learn each subject. As a teacher both are prerequisites for the children in your class to be active learners.

Teach children how to learn   This means the internal dialogue that goes on when anyone learns anything is important. Making this explicit to your children is really important. They need to know that talking about what they are learning is part of the learning process. They need to know that 'talking in the head' (metacognition) is part of the learning process. Working in pairs and small groups to solve particular problems is a powerful way of modelling this. You need to be able to help them know how subjects work; you'll want to explore with them all the things that make each distinctive, for example, the language of the topic, its concepts, theory, philosophy, processes and procedures.

Links

Feedback
Formative assessment
Independent learning
Learning styles
Recording individual progress
Self-assessment by pupils
Subject knowledge
Summative assessment
Thinking skills

Strategies

To enable active learning:
Before beginning a new topic:

- check what each child knows about the topic;
- know the common preconceptions and possible misconceptions about the topic.

In your preparation ensure that you:

- are providing factually accurate knowledge;
- understand the facts and ideas within a conceptual framework;
- know which areas might be hard to learn;
- organize what you teach to make it easy to recall and use.

In each session:

- clearly define learning goals with the children;
- use small steps and really carefully chosen examples to make the 'hard to grasp' easy to learn;
- keep checking what has been understood;
- tell children what they have learnt about the topic;
- tell them what else they need to do to learn about the topic;
- tell children about the ways in which they have been successful as learners;
- give them something more to work on to be even more successful learners.

Development

Our understanding about active learning for children is based on a science of learning. Each of these headings provides its theoretical underpinning. They are starting places for developing a deeper understanding about active learning:

a. Memory and the structure of knowledge.
b. Problem solving and reasoning.
c. Early foundations of learning.
d. Regulatory processes that govern learning (including metacognition). This is about how the brain learns.
e. Symbolic thinking and culture and the learning community.

Further reading

Whitehead, D. (Ed.) (2000) *The Psychology of Teaching and Learning in the Primary School*, London: Routledge/Falmer. Section II: 'Teaching the Curriculum' is a starting place for exploring these ideas'.

Banks, F. and Shelton Mayes, A. (Eds) (2001) *Early Professional Development for Teachers*, London: Open University/David Fulton. Section 2 'Teaching for learning' has some useful chapters.

National Research Council (2000) *How People Learn*, Washington: National Academic Press. Seminal US report that used extensive review of available research to make statements about learning and teaching.

Sousa, D. A. (2001) *How the Brain Learns: A Classroom Teacher's Guide*, 2nd edn, Thousand Oaks: Corwin. A really practical guide on how to improve your teaching and children's learning through understanding how the brain works.

TTA Standards
1.2, 3.3.3.

Assessment

See entries: Baseline assessment, Feedback, Formative assessment, Summative assessment, Self-assessment by pupils

Baseline assessment

The term baseline assessment is applicable for any assessment which is used as a starting point or first measure of a child's knowledge. In England, the term is particularly used for the testing that takes place when a child first enters the formal education system at the age of 4 or 5 years. Each school is required to make a simple assessment of basic skills. This assessment is then used to set targets for children's educational development in class. In England the results are also used to set school targets for the end of Key Stage 1. Baseline assessment varies from school to school and authority to authority. There is no national scheme in place but the baseline assessment used has to be one which has been approved by the Qualifications and Curriculum Authority (QCA).

Links
Early learning goals
Formative assessment
Research and its uses
Summative assessment

Strategies
- Make yourself familiar with the baseline assessment in place in your school.
- Find out how the results are used.

Development

Baseline assessment is used in research to establish a starting point of what pupils can do before a research project takes place, where learning is involved. Often a 'control' group is also assessed so that when both groups are re-tested at the end of the teaching input, any added value can be established. Sometimes just the research group is tested and then their acquired knowledge is mapped against their previous knowledge.

Class teachers sometimes make initial assessments before teaching a topic to inform them which aspects to focus on. Some teachers employ 'concept mapping' where the children themselves identify what they know about a topic. Either of these activities could be encompassed by the term baseline assessment because they measure knowledge prior to teaching activity.

Further reading

The QCA website has the most up-to-date information
http//: www.qca.org.uk/ca/foundation

TTA Standards

3.2.1, 3.2.3.

Behaviour

See *Discipline*.

Bullying

It is useful to think of bullying or harassment as a particular type of aggressive behaviour. The bully intends to hurt the victim. The hurt can be physical or psychological, or both. When children open up about this they emphasize the effects of bullying. There is no doubt that victims get extremely distressed. Bullying is generally thought to have three characteristics:

- It is unprovoked.
- It occurs repeatedly.
- The bully is stronger, or thought to be stronger, than the victim.

Bullying is repeated action; a one-off incident, whilst unpleasant, isn't bullying. More than once is enough to take serious action. Usually bullying takes the following forms:

physical aggression – being hit;
verbal aggression – name calling;
indirect – being ignored, left out, nasty looks.

Anyone, or any group, who finds that he/she/they can get a response by using aggression, can bully. Often the bully will have a gang who support tacitly, if not actively. It is difficult to detect, as bullying doesn't go on in the teacher's sight. Most bullying in school is well hidden and disguised. Most bullies will vehemently deny involvement in bullying. Whilst obvious victims are children who are different, either physically, emotionally, or intellectually, unfortunately, if the circumstances are right, any child can be a victim. Some English research has suggested that 1 in 4 children of primary age are bullied more than once or twice in any one term. Bullied children may be very reluctant to tell as often they think it is their own fault. Victims may blame themselves, they quickly lose self-confidence and self-esteem. They will find it difficult to concentrate. Some will take time off from school to avoid being bullied. They may achieve less well than predicted.

Links

Child protection
Communication with parents
Communication about learning
Discipline
Emotional development
Equal opportunities
Purposeful working atmosphere
Social development
Values and ethos

Strategies

This has to be dealt with through a whole school approach; parents and all the adults in the school and all the children need to be involved. It should be made a high priority. In the school:

- Everyone should know what bullying is and what to do if they become aware it is happening.

- Monitoring of bullying should be going on. Anonymous questionnaires are an effective means of collecting this data.
- Free time, between lessons and in the school grounds, needs active supervision, with a range of activities to keep children happily engaged and a support network for children who experience bullying.
- Displaying helpline posters will help children who find it most difficult to tell.
- All children will be encouraged to take positive action against bullying.

In your classroom prevention should be the key, teach how to:

- Build co-operative relationships with other children through group activities and a variety of pairings, etc.
- Resist bullying behaviour through role-play, peer discussion, the choice of stories to be read aloud, etc.
- Develop alternatives to aggression, with the children, as a means of sorting differences through modelling, discussion and role-play.

Development

Bullying and harassment can be real barriers to learning. This is one very good reason to make sure that it is always taken seriously. Teachers need to encourage children to tell an adult if they are being bullied, or if they know someone who is being bullied. This means that what bullying is, and what it isn't, has to be talked about regularly and frequently. Teachers need to be vigilant for signs of bullying; they should always investigate suspected incidents promptly. Parents need to be involved at an early stage. To achieve change, a problem-solving approach, working with both victim and bully to make the situation clear, can often work. It is your job to follow up on all incidents, to make sure that bullying is not resumed.

Further reading

Department for Education (DfE) (1994) *Bullying: Don't Suffer in Silence. An Anti Bullying Pack for Schools*, London: DfE.

Mosely, J. (1994) *Turn your School Around*, Cambridge: LDA.

Smith, P. K. and Sharp, S. (1993) *School Bullying: Insights and Perspectives*, London: Routledge.

The following webpages are useful on anti bullying:

http://www.antibullying.net/

http://www.bullying.co.uk/
http://www.scre.ac.uk/bully/index.html

TTA Standard
3.3.14.

Challenge

See *Expectations about pupils' Learning.*

Child development

Some aspects of development are obvious. As you look at children in the playground you spot that younger children are not as physically developed as older children. The questions teachers need to answer are about when and how children acquire all sorts of skills and knowledge. There are many models about development. Some models assume that change is continuous. In these there is an expectation that all 7-year-olds will be able to, for example, skip. Development is continuous, gradual and inevitable, it is orderly and smooth. Discontinuous development would suggest that there is a stage when everything is in place for the child to be able to skip. This view sees development as ragged and uneven. In the example, children would learn to skip if all those things that enable skipping to happen were in place: wanting to skip, having someone to help, as well as all the other physical attributes such as, balance, skeletal strength and muscle development. It might hold that most 7-year-olds will be able to skip, but some children can skip at a much younger age and others will be much older. All models attempt to account for stability and change. In considering temperament, for example, is an outgoing child always going to be that way (is this stable?) or will the outgoingness change over time (is it unstable?). Thinkers about development are also interested in the extent to which heritability (what comes from the inherited genes) and environment interact. These questions are about how you make the most of what you are born with.

There may be important periods where some learning is most easily accomplished. If these milestones have been missed, then schooling has to offer the opportunity for catching up. For example, motor skills, learning to walk, run, jump, may be best accomplished in the first six years (see *Physical development*).

Young children need to have the opportunity to develop physical skills in school. Emotional control (see *Emotional development*) can be learned after the 'terrible twos' but may need more help right through the years at school. It may be sensible to use the developing brain capacity (see *Intellectual development*) to acquire language from 0–12 years, to include both first and additional language teaching at this age (see *Linguistic development*). It certainly seems to be more difficult to become proficient in an additional language if teaching is delayed until 13. This means that teachers have to take account of individual development to ensure that teaching and learning are effective.

Links

Emotional development
Intellectual development
Linguistic development
Physical development
Social development

Further reading

Keenan, T. (2002) *An Introduction to Child Development*, London: Sage.
   This is an example of many books about development.

Child protection

Child protection is to do with the role that the school has in keeping the child safe. In an educational setting, the 'child' will include anyone who is not legally an adult. A particular UK example is The Children Act, 1989. This came about through a growing awareness of child abuse and a determination to do something to protect children and young people. The key principles of the Act are:

- The child is a person and not an object of concern.
- Parents are entitled to be treated with greater respect and to be kept more fully informed.
- Statutory powers should be used only when necessary and last for the minimum time possible.
- Careful consideration should be given to the operation of inter-agency procedures.

In the statutory framework:

- The child's welfare is of 'paramount consideration'.
- Delay is likely to be prejudicial to the child and should be avoided.
- Courts should not make care orders unless it is clear that to do so would be better for the child than not doing so.
- Decisions should be made in partnership with the child and his/ her parents or carers wherever possible.
- Children have a right to be consulted and listened to when decisions are being made about their lives.

Both the principles and the law are similar in other countries. As in England and Wales, in many other countries the education service is part of the inter-agency approach. This means that teachers act not as individuals but as part of a shared approach. Most teachers are not qualified nor authorized to sort out child abuse. But they need to recognize and report suspected abuse. In England and Wales teachers report to the named person within the school (every school has a designated senior member of staff, often the head). This person receives training for the role.

Categories of abuse/identification

A child is considered to be abused or at risk of abuse, by parents or other carers, when the basic needs of the child are not being met through avoidable acts either of commission or omission. This means that a parent may be doing something horrid to the child or may be neglecting to do something, for example, not providing regular food. To make these judgements, knowing what the developmental milestones are is important knowledge for you. You should know the physical and mental stages that children and adolescents go through.

Physical injury

Remember that parenting is very hard work. From time to time parents walk to the edge of a metaphorical cliff, and, infuriated beyond control by their off-spring, unfortunately some fall off. Be open-minded, but be vigilant. Not everything is wickedness, but not everything is innocent either.

For example, consider:

- Black eyes – one occasionally is an accident, two may be an indication that a child has been hit deliberately, i.e. a non-accidental injury.
- Bruising – the shape of the bruise is important, if you saw eight round bruises on either side of a child's back and two on either side of the ribs, it might be a game where someone, entirely innocently, throws the child in the air and catches them. But it might be that the child has been shaken.
- Round burns anywhere indicate cigarette burns and, without doubt, are something that should be further investigated.

Neglect/failure to thrive

- For example, consider a pupil who loses weight during a school holiday.

Emotional abuse

- For example, consider the child who is obsessively good in your class. He/she may be in a home environment of low warmth and high criticism, and is afraid to get things wrong.

Sexual abuse

- For example consider a 5-year-old who knows the names of genitals and plays sexy games with dolls or other children. It is really hard to make this judgement. Be grateful that there are staff in school who will take this responsibility – but only if you tell them about it.

It is important to get abuse into perspective by knowing that it is comparatively rare. In England, 32 children in every 10,000 (1994 figures) were considered to have been abused. It is possible to go through a working life and never come across an abused child.

Links

Bullying
Discipline
Emotional development
Intellectual development
Linguistic development

Physical development
Relationships with pupils
Social development
Working with other adults

Strategies

What do you do? What is your duty of care?

- Take responsibility to teach about abuse and other issues that are about safety, e.g. bullying.
- Help children to know when to tell an adult about a concern.
- Have a classroom that is high on warmth, low on criticism.
- Develop trust between you and those you teach.
- If you suspect non-accidental physical damage or any other form of abuse, don't panic. Respond promptly and professionally – know the codes of conduct and procedures for your school – be careful to apply them. Be aware that you cannot promise the child not to tell. In incidents of abuse you may not offer confidentiality to the child. It is better to take action that later has a reasonable explanation than to have a child suffer.
- Don't make a drama out of a crisis. Act on a 'need to know' basis. Only tell the people who are responsible for taking further action.
- As soon as you can, WRITE DOWN time, place, people, context. If matters go to court you will need a written record of the actions you took.
- If things look as if they may go to law, don't be your own lawyer, use support services.

Further reading

Used with caution, the World Wide Web is a sensible way to further research this area, because it gives access to up-to-date information. Most teachers' professional organizations and unions have access to expert advice on all aspects of child protection and other child safety issues. For example, www.data.teachers.org.uk gets you to the National Union of Teachers' site.

DfEE Circular 10/95 *Protecting Children from Abuse: The Role of the Education Service*, www.dfee.gov.uk/circulars/10_95/summary.htm This sets out what to do in English schools. Other countries will have similar procedural instruments.

www.baspcan.org.uk/child_protect.htm   This is a useful website with links to organizations worldwide with a concern for child safety.

DfEE Circular 4/95 *Drugs Prevention and Schools,* www.dfee.gov.uk/circulars/4_95/summary.htm This sets out what English schools are expected to do about illegal drugs and tobacco and solvent abuse.

TTA Standard

1.8.

Code of Practice

This is a brief summary of some aspects of the Special Educational Needs Code of Practice, as it applies to schools in England.

The definition of Special Educational Needs

Children with Special Educational Needs (SEN) have learning difficulties that need special provision, for example:

a. difficulties in learning, significantly greater than the majority of children at the same age; or
b. have a disability which prevents or hinders them from making use of educational facilities of a kind generally provided for children of the same age in schools within the area of the local educational authority.

(Section 312, Education Act, 1996)

There is provision under the 1996 Education Act for children who are not yet school age to have their needs recognized and met.

Further definitions of SEN come from the Children Act, 1989, (Section 17(11)). These include children with disabilities such as 'blind, deaf or dumb or suffers from mental disorder of any kind or is substantially and permanently handicapped by illness, injury or congenital deformity or such other disability as may be prescribed' (Children Act, 1989).

Disabilities Discrimination Act, 1995 (Section 1(1)) adds children with disabilities that have a 'substantial or long term adverse effect . . . on . . . day-to-day activities' to the list of definitions.

The Code of Practice (CoP) sets out some principles

The CoP states that a child with SEN should have his/her needs met, normally in mainstream schools.

A child with SEN should have his/her views sought and taken into account. The parent's role in supporting the education of their child is recognized as vital.

A child with SEN should have access to a broad, balanced and relevant curriculum (for both the foundation stage, i.e. 3–5 years and National Curriculum, i.e. 5 years old and beyond).

Some of the success criteria in the CoP

The plan for each child identifies the ways that all a child's needs are met, taking account of cultural needs, management needs and the way resources are best used in schools, that SEN pupils are identified early, and that 'best practice' is exploited. The child's wishes and the parent's views should be taken into account. The assessment of need is within prescribed time limits. Statements about each child are clear, detailed and time limited, the monitoring is specified and annually reviewed. It is expected that if the parents and the child want him/her to be educated in a mainstream school, that this will happen. At the same time, the CoP recognizes that a very small number of children have conditions so severe as to make this impractical. Some specialist provision will remain.

Under the CoP, *parents* are expected to be actively involved in the decisions made about their child. Account has to be taken of their views, attitudes, emotional investment and differing perspectives about the process, the child, the people involved and the range of provision. The parents' needs have to be met in setting up meetings, when these are and where they are held should be convenient for them. They must be told when a SEN is first identified for their child. They must be kept informed throughout schooling and involved in decision making. They have duties and responsibilities as well.

Pupils have to be involved in decisions made about them. Account has to be taken about their age, maturity and capability when doing this. They must 'not be overburdened when they have insufficient experience knowledge and without additional support' (Children Act, 1989/Chidren with Disabilities, 1991 regulations). They are to be involved both in Individual Educational Plans (IEP) made for them and in the assessment process. As they get towards the end of schooling they are expected to start to take a lead role in what they are going to do with the rest of their lives.

In early years settings (i.e. before school at age 5 years) there is an emphasis on early identification of need. The adoption of a 'graduated approach' is expected. Early Years' Action (EYA) includes this cycle:

identifying the need;
doing what seems best to meet that need;
assessing progress;
stopping when the need is successfully met.

If it is not, EYA continues going through the cycle again, trying different approaches. If the child is not making adequate progress under EYA, this triggers outside advice and support: Early Years' Action Plus (EYA+) with, for under 5s, informal assessment every 6 months and, at age 5, detailed information to parents to inform transfer decisions. If the child is in school the Special Needs Co-ordinator (SENCO, see below) takes these actions. In other settings it will be someone with day-to-day contact with the child.

Schools (from age 5) use information that already exists with a focus of 'can do' and 'needs to learn'. This action will use baseline assessment and other tests to make judgements about need. During schooling, the teachers will use ongoing observations, assessment and feedback in planning to meet needs. Joint home school learning approaches will be encouraged. Differentiation is assumed to be happening for *all* the children in school. In the School Action (SA) phase a 'graduated approach' continues in the way outlined for EYA. If the child is not making sufficient progress, then the school will move to School Action Plus (SA+). SA+ may include the writing of an Individual Education Plan (IEP) where differentiation is over and above what would normally be expected. The advice of specialists and resources from beyond the school may be used. Parents and pupil involvement remains active.

The CoP has provision to include early or interim reports sent for *children at risk of serious disaffection or exclusion.* These children can be dealt with under SA and SA+.

English as an additional language is not equated with SEN although it is recognized as requiring extra resources.

The curriculum for SEN children must use work from earlier Key Stages to allow pupils to demonstrate progress and attainment.

LEAs (Local Education Authorities) are to have a common style in all schools for EYA/SA and EYA+/SA+. Each child with SEN has an *annual review.* This is done within the school. LEAs are responsible for reminding schools which children should be reviewed each term.

In Year 9, a link is made with Connexions (see *Connexions*) for all students (a multi-agency service for young people). As with all students, this is to help the student with SEN to make decisions about what to do at the end of school years. Connexions will add information to the annual review. By Year 11 the annual review will have much more involvement of agencies beyond the school. The review must be sent by the school to the LEA within 10 working days.

The Special Educational Needs Co-ordinator (SENCO) has a significant role in all this. It is strategic, determining policy and whole school approaches to teaching and learning for children with SEN. It requires significant time to fulfil the role. In a school with many children with barriers to learning, it may leave time for no other duties. It has status, the SENCO is a senior manager with a special role in communication with colleagues, parents and pupils, and with those beyond the school. Part of the CoP is concerned with training and improving skills for both the SENCO and all those working with children with SEN. In some secondary schools the SENCO will manage a large department with teachers and learning assistants and hold resources for children with SEN.

Some children, even after SA and SA+, still don't make much progress. For these pupils the SENCO, in consultation with colleagues, or parents and the child, or an outside agency, will start the *statutory assessment* process. Significant cause for concern will only trigger a request for statutory assessment when outcomes of EYA/SA and EYA+/SA+ are demonstrated. There will be many children in EYA/SA and EYA+/SA+, but comparatively few will require statutory assessment. This is the point at which LEA decisions become important. Children whose needs are assessed will not automatically be granted a statement. The school, parents and child may be asked to go back to EYA+/SA+, with perhaps more support. Statements, once written, generate additional LEA support and use centrally held resources (i.e. specialist staff). There has to be a prompt and flexible response to newly identified needs. The *statement* must be a precise description of provision for the child with SEN. Some children have needs identified at a very early age. They have statements before they start formal education.

In the CoP it is expected that LEA and schools will work in partnership. They are expected to use their best endeavours to meet needs, to find cost effective solutions, to provide information about mainstream provision for parents, to enable assessment to add knowledge about the child with SEN and to ensure that mainstream education is the norm.

Links

Connexions
Inclusion
Special Educational Needs

Further reading

Department for Education and Skills (DfES) (2001) *Special Educational Needs: Code of Practice*, London: DfES (581/2001). This document has all the details not included in the summary above. It is well worth reading the sections that apply to the age range you teach.

TTA Standard

2.6.

Communicating clearly

Communicating clearly is an essential skill for the teacher. This involves what you have to say and how you say it. Talking to large groups is not a skill we use in everyday life, so it has to be learned. First, when planning to talk to the whole class, or the whole school, consider carefully the points you wish to convey. If necessary, jot key words and phrases down on a lesson plan or a small card. This will enable you to be succinct and talk to your audience rather than read to them.

During a lesson a teacher uses different voices rather like an actor. To gain attention your voice needs to be loud and firm. It is best to keep the attention gaining instruction short, loud enough to be heard by all, and to use a familiar phrase such as 'Stop what you are doing, and look this way'. When attention is gained you can switch to a style appropriate to what you have to say. This might be an instructional style or a conversational style, but it will be quieter so that the children have to listen and will not feel that they can both talk to their friends and listen to you!

Whilst the children are working, you will be moving round the room or working with a group and your voice will be much quieter. Occasionally you will scan the room and may use short commands or name children whose attention you want to attract.

This indicates to the whole class that you are aware of them all, even though you are engaged directly with only a few. Sometimes you can praise a child in a loud voice which others can hear. This can make the child feel good and others want to work harder so that they can be praised too. If most 'loud' comments in the lesson are either instructional or positive a better classroom atmosphere is created.

Finally, expression and variation in your voice is important. All of us like to listen to actors and story-tellers. Teachers need to be a little bit of an actor and story-teller to motivate and convey enthusiasm for topics. Learn to use different tones to convey your expectations. After all, you cannot really get cross every time a child does something silly, but you can sound cross so that they know they have crossed the line of acceptability.

Links
Behaviour
Communication about learning
Discipline
Instruction
Purposeful working atmosphere
Whole class teaching

Strategies
- Work out what you will say to the whole class.
- Plan using phrases rather than whole sentences, so that you can talk rather than read.
- Have a set phrase that gains attention and gives instruction, so that the children have no choice but to pay attention.
- Make inputs interesting by using a variety of tones of voice.
- Keep instructions short and clear.
- Use the tone of your voice to indicate your approval or disapproval.
- Be clear with young children in what you say and how you say it.
- Use words and phrases and mannerisms to the whole class to establish 'presence'.
- Try and maintain a 'positive' classroom atmosphere.

Development
Teachers have different views on how to communicate with children. Wells (1996) summarizes a study on young children's meaning,

making important conclusions on how teachers facilitate high quality conversation and guide children to reinvent knowledge. He contrasts these situations with a traditional transmission style of teaching where the teacher imparts the knowledge and the children are expected to listen and learn.

Communication can be more than oral comment. Cruickshank *et al.* (1979) surveyed students with the research question 'Clear teaching, what is it?'. The results were summarized into the following eight responses:

1. Gives us a chance to think about what's being taught.
2. Explains something and then stops so we can think about it.
3. Shows us how to remember things.
4. Gives us enough time for practice.
5. Teaches at a pace appropriate to the topic and pupils.
6. Takes time when explaining.
7. Answers pupils' questions.
8. Stresses difficult points.

Further reading

Cruickshank, D., Kennedy, J., Bush, A. and Myers, B. (1979) 'Clear teaching – what is it?', *British Journal of Teacher Education*, 5: 1, (27–33).

Wells, G. (1996) 'Conversation and the reinvention of knowledge' in Pollard, A. *Readings for Reflective Teaching in the Primary School*, London: Cassell.

TTA Standard

3.2.7.

Communication about learning

If children are to learn actively, then your feedback on how they're doing is extremely important. The relationship between you and those who you teach needs to be positive. If you are high on warmth (empathy) and low on criticism, this creates an ethos that is nurturing and will enable each child to do well. During the time you spend with your class you will learn about progress and achievement in many aspects of each child's life. You will learn what makes them happy and what makes them sad in their life outside school. Yard (playground) duty, and other 'informal' responsibilities, including extra curricular clubs and sport, are all important in getting to really know something about those whom you teach.

Links

Active learning
Communicating clearly
Culture
Differentiation
Expectations about pupils' learning
Feedback
Independent learning
Listening and responding to pupils
Motivation
Relationships with pupils
Self-assessment by pupils
Target setting
Values and ethos

Strategies

Make accurate assessments about:

- the learning process – how does the child learn?
- progress towards learning objectives – what the child is learning?

Ask the child:

- how he/she learns;
- about achievement.

Tell the child:

- how you think he/she learns;
- about the progress towards the learning objective that he/she is making;
- success in both the learning process and the learning objectives.

Set realistic targets for improving:

- the way the child learns;
- achievement.

Both written and verbal comments should start with the positive, 'you've worked hard', 'you've really grasped this', before setting targets.

Make communication two-way, ask:

- how do you feel you've got on?
- how did you do that?
- what do you think you need to do to improve?

Help the child to set realistic and achievable goals for him/herself – targets have to challenge, but they also have to be realistic and achievable.

Development

The focus is on the learning and tasks that the child does. When they do less well, rather than blaming the children, it is about improving their work. When they do well, it is about telling them that the work is good. You will also comment on how they did the work. This places the emphasis on communicating about the process and products of learning. This approach is thought to increase motivation and to reduce the incidence of disaffection. The long-term aim is to make children able to identify when they have done well and when they could do better, for themselves.

The reason for the strategies and the emphasis on what the child achieves is based on research about how learners think about success. Some put success down to luck, some to ability and some to effort. The three explanations have different outcomes. They should lead to a differentiated feedback to those who you teach. For example, if success is down to ability then if I do better:

it might be that I've been lucky; or it might be that I've worked harder.

Either way 'doing better', I may think, is beyond my control. My teacher can help with this by helping me to think strategically. The questions, 'how did you do that?' and 'what do you think you need to do to improve?' are particularly useful for learners like this.

Further reading

Chaplian, R. (2000) 'Helping children to persevere and be well motivated', in Whitebread, D. (Ed.) *The Psychology of Teaching and Learning in the Primary School*, London: Routledge, is a useful introduction to these ideas.

TTA Standard

3.2.7.

Communication with parents

Parents, the people who care for the pupils in your class, have rights and responsibilities. Your respect for them is central to establishing and maintaining a working relationship.

Partnership with parents, in helping their children to become successful at school and beyond, can be achieved in many ways. With younger children contact is frequent, often on a daily basis, when someone brings and collects the child. As the child becomes more independent contact needs to rely more on formal meetings. The social events that schools put on are hugely important in building relationships. The effort put into this aspect of schooling is important because it builds bridges and helps communication. However, it should always be remembered that the power relationships between teacher and parents mean that partnership is likely to be uneven, (for example, in school, it's you who holds the position of power – you're 'the teacher', but on home territory, the parent is the main decision maker).

Links

Culture
Ethnicity
Homework
Parents
Special Educational Needs
Values and ethos

Strategies

- Build your reputation as a trustworthy and reliable authority by being positive and helpful.
- Prepare for meetings (both informal and formal) and written reports, which needs:
  - accurate information about the progress the child is making;
  - knowing about the child, both in the class setting and beyond, their behaviour, talents, ambitions and difficulties.

Be:

- Approachable – in face-to-face meetings, smile and be pleasant; in written reports use a style that is accessible to your audience.
- A good listener to what is said and to what is meant – sometimes parents are less than direct about a worry they have.
- Responsive.

- Considerate and polite.
- Serious.
- Constructive.
- Both honest and tactful.
- Well presented – both in person and in what you write.

Development

The idea of partnership, of a shared interest, is a key to success in teacher/parent working relationships. Partnerships between parents and teachers may be at several levels. In some schools there is a real sharing of responsibility for pupils' progress. Parents will be well-informed about academic, social and other aspects of their child's progress in school. They'll be active in informing teachers about things at home that may influence learning in school. Other parents will also be well-informed but perhaps less confident, less concerned and less willing to share information with teachers. Some parents are happiest to leave decisions to the teachers. This does not mean that they are not concerned about their child's welfare, just that they see teachers as not requiring their input. Some parents, and these are a concern, are uninvolved, and seem very hard to reach. However, most teachers have very comfortable and useful contacts with parents. This is not necessarily a full partnership. One reason for this is that teachers are often wary that parental influence may become interference. This may be true for parents too, who do not wish to reveal their home circumstances to teachers.

Further reading

Cowley, S. (1999) *Starting Teaching: How to Succeed and Survive*, London: Cassell, Chapter 11, 'Parents', deals with how to manage this aspect of your work.

Hughes, P. (2000) *Principles of Primary Education – Study Guide*, London: David Fulton, Chapter 10 'Home–School–Community Connections', useful suggestions on parental help in and out of school.

Thody, A., Gray, B. and Bowden, D. (2000) *The Teacher's Survival Guide*, London: Continuum, Chapter 7, 'Significant others', is another guide on what and how to do this.

TTA Standards

1.4, 3.2.7.

Competition

Competition is part of our society and education system (exams, grades, sports). Competition need not exclude intrinsic reward but you need to be clear about its place in the culture of your classroom.

'Competition is good for you' and 'The World is a competitive place', are two frequently heard slogans. As with all enduring slogans there is probably some truth in them. If you are able to compete, competition can be enjoyable. If you have a chance of winning, it is a highly motivating activity. It does not take long for children to work out what their individual or team chances are. Then either they will continue to compete because they conform to what is expected of them, or they become completely de-motivated and cease to take part. If they do not join in this can be infuriating for other team members and sometimes peer pressure is successfully brought to bear.

With these thoughts in mind, you need to think carefully about the competition you offer in the classroom. Most children seek to achieve house points, stars, teacher's approval, smiley stamps, work on the wall, all of which are forms of reward. Children themselves often turn some of these into competitive situations. For example, 'I've got two pictures on the wall, you haven't got any'. As the teacher, if you create a competitive situation, will success be accessible to all the competitors? Are there situations where reward is intrinsic? This means pupils are participating because they want to and they care about the quality of the product, or they see there is a purposeful objective. If there are no rewards on offer will the children engage/behave? You and the children need to be clear about these procedures so that they can learn about their own motivations.

Links

Active learning
Bullying
Discipline
Independent learning
Motivation
Rewards
Standardized tests
Summative assessment

Strategies

- Is it appropriate to make this activity competitive?
- Can all the children participating see that they can have some form of success?
- Is the reward suitable?
- Are the rules clear to all participants?
- How are you developing intrinsic motivation?

Development

Every teacher wants the children in their class to be well motivated and most teachers spend time looking for something that will motivate even the most reluctant learner. Competition is a powerful motivator but it does not work for everyone. One can consider competing against others or oneself. The choice to participate or not lies with the pupil, whatever pressure is brought to bear, be it punishment or reward. For the teacher it is a delicate mix between preparing children for an education system, which predominantly measures success by examination achievements, and developing a desire within children to do tasks because they are innately interesting or beneficial.

Muijs and Reynolds (2001) describe work carried out by Borich in 1996 in which he describes three types of classroom, the competitive, the co-operative and the individualistic. In the competitive classroom the standards are set by the teacher, pupils give right or wrong responses, as judged by the teacher, and pupils have a sense of success or failure set against the achievement or non-achievement of these targets. In contrast the individualistic classroom encourages more independent decision making, targets are set by the students themselves and the teacher operates more in a guidance mode. Incidentally, in general, boys prefer the competitive classroom.

Further reading

Borich, G. (1996) *Effective Teaching Methods*, 3rd edn, New York: Macmillan.

Muijs, D. and Reynolds, D. (2001) *Effective Teaching: Evidence and Practice*, London: Paul Chapman.

Completed work

Children should complete their work. If the work is important, it is important enough to complete. It is a good habit to learn to complete tasks. Some schools have this expectation written into their teaching and learning policy.

When a child is not completing work it might be because they are off task and more interested in something else going on in the classroom. It might be that:

- something is wrong at home or socially and they cannot concentrate;
- that the work is too hard and they cannot get started and therefore do not complete in the time given;
- they are a slow worker;
- they are poor at listening to instructions;
- you have set them too much to do;
- the child does not see the purpose of the work set;
- you have set the same amount of work to children who have different abilities or different speeds of working.

Responding appropriately to a pupil with incomplete work depends on the cause. If you have set an unreasonable amount, then it seems tough to keep children in at playtime to finish it or ask them to complete it at home. On the other hand, if the child has been 'messing about' then action ought to be taken. First decide on the cause. Then decide on an appropriate action.

If you allow work to be completed at home, some children may take the opportunity to socialize in your lesson and choose to do the work at home when they are on their own. Giving 'finishing off' as homework is not recommended by the DfES (www.dfes.gov.uk).

Links

Differentiation
Homework
Independent learning
Listening and responding to pupils
Special Educational Needs

Strategies

- Set amounts which can reasonably be completed by individuals.
- Use shorter tasks and let children move on to the next step if there is time.

- Set out clearly, at the start, what you expect to be completed and remind them of this goal at regular intervals.
- Try and differentiate the amount given to match the ability of the child.
- Help poor starters to get going.
- Set quick finishers more complex and demanding tasks about the same topic.

Development

When children enter employment they will be expected to complete all tasks, therefore it is appropriate to develop this work habit. With more support and control to start with, you should be able to make completion of work a high probability. Gradually, children can be asked to make judgements about how long they think they will take, how long they need to complete a task and eventually to organize parts of their own timetable with less rigorous supervision. This is part of the move towards developing independent learning and working skills. It is important to allow these decision making opportunities in appropriate situations. You never know, when they have a place of their own, even the DIY jobs may all get completed!

Connexions

In English secondary education this is a new inter-agency approach which will have an impact on the inclusion agenda. Connexions is a single point of access for *all* 13–19-year-olds to help to prepare for the transition to work and adult life.

Links
Code of Practice
Inclusion
Special Educational Needs

Consolidation

Consolidation is allowing time and opportunity for learning to take place. Not many people have the ability to remember everything they are told first time round. Children need varying amounts of practice at a topic before it is secure in their minds. The advantage of revisiting work in slightly different contexts also allows children to see the commonalties in more abstract ideas and enables them to deepen their concepts. This hopefully will lead to them transferring the ideas to new, similar situations.

Links
Able children
Active learning
Differentiation
Lesson plan structure
Medium-term planning
Special Educational Needs

Strategies
- Allow time in medium- and short-term planning for children to revisit and explore new learning.
- Consider carefully whether consolidation for particular pupils needs to be in the same context or can it be a new context (in which will the best learning take place?).

Development
Consolidation serves two purposes. First, it allows children to experience similar learning in different contexts and therefore expands their understanding of the learning and how it might look in different guises. This may even facilitate the ability to recognize where old knowledge can be applied in new situations (transfer). Second, it allows for practice. Rather like the number of driving lessons you need, we all need different amounts of practice before we feel secure in a new skill. We also need to try out our driving skills in different road and traffic conditions. This is an analogy for the need to place learning in different contexts, so that children can exercise their acquired skills.

Continuing professional development (CPD)

Throughout your teaching career your professional development needs will be met in a variety of ways. Your opportunities for school funding are most likely to be met where your needs are closely aligned with those identified for school-wide improvement. Some, perhaps most, of what you need, will be acquired in your school and local area. You will work with experienced colleagues for example, to:

- manage your class effectively;
- differentiate your teaching to include all pupils;
- develop the curriculum;
- meet targets for public accountability.

Provision for continuing professional development (CPD) beyond the school may be met in a variety of ways. This will include membership of professional associations, including teacher unions, local courses run for groups of schools on particular aspects of teaching and the curriculum. If you are ambitious and academically minded, education departments at your local university will offer post-graduate studies, including masters degrees and doctorates. These may have a subject, or an age phase, or special needs, or management focus. It's often possible to build your own course from units and modules of work that have a particular appeal to you, and to spread the work over several years. In England, the DfES offers grants for aspects of CPD, including bursaries for those in their second and third years of teaching.

Links
Part One
Research and its uses
Teachers' employment and conditions

Strategies
- Have a clear set of targets for your professional development.
- Evaluate your progress towards targets against a realistic time scale.
- Identify what you think you to need to learn:
  - if this aligns with the school improvement plan, take part in staff development provided;
  - if it is a personal professional development target, seek other ways of meeting this.

Development
These days it makes sense to have a career plan. In England, automatic annual pay rises can no longer be taken for granted.

Teachers are subject to performance management procedures. These will monitor individual professional development. This means that thinking about where you want to be and what you want to be doing is strongly recommended. You may want to be the best teacher ever, or you may want to be a manager, or work to support particular groups of pupils, or you may want to change to another career. Have a plan, even if you later find that you take a different route.

Further reading

These books will help you to think about teaching as a career:

Bubb, S. and Hoare, P. (2001) *Performance Management Monitoring Teaching in the Primary School*, London: David Fulton.

http://www.teachernet.gov.uk   The DfES is a possible source of CPD funding.

Cowley, S. (1999) *Starting Teaching, How to Succeed and Survive*, London: Continuum.

Thody, A., Gray, B. and Bowden, D. (2000) *The Teacher's Survival Guide*, London: Continuum.

TAA Standard

1.7.

Culture

Culture is determined by the set(s) of values and experiences and traditions that individuals and groups hold. Cultural groups may be determined, for example, by language, forms of dress, ethical and religious beliefs, diet and customs. As a teacher, you will have a set of expectations about the children you teach. Some of these result from your own cultural heritage and the traditions you and your family and community has. Your awareness about other cultural groups will inform your teaching. Knowing about different cultures means that you can choose methods, resources and examples that will help your learners. It also helps to avoid misunderstandings. For example, you may think that a child who has misbehaved is being defiant because as you tell him/her off there in no eye contact. In some cultures children know that it is rude to look an adult in the eye, especially when you're displeased with them. The child you think defiant, may be using home rules to avert your displeasure.

Links

Communication with parents
English as an additional language
Equal opportunities
Ethnicity
Relationships with pupils
Resources
Social development
Values and ethos

Strategies

Find out about the culture of those who you teach:

- ask the children;
- talk to parents;
- use the expertise of school staff;
- find out about the community the school serves.

Respect cultural difference, take care:

- over the language you use;
- to choose teaching methods and resources that are appropriate for the cultural mix in your class;
- that your stereotypes, useful as they are, may need to be re-examined from time to time.

Celebrate cultural richness (but avoid tokenism).

Development

This entry has over-simplified a complex concept. Culture is not a fixed entity. A great many things influence individuals. Their cultural group is only one factor. A social justice agenda would place much more emphasis on the nuances of difference and equality. In the UK in 2002, there is political debate about citizenship and what this is. Understanding culture, with associated ideas about tolerance, politics, conflict resolution and moral reasoning, will help to inform your opinion about this. The emotional capital invested in national identity is complex. Ethnicity is part of this. In England, though the majority of people are white, there are Asian, Black and other minority ethnic groups in the population. Each of these groups and sub-groups has a cultural identity. In some cultures, the roles that men and women take are fairly clearly determined. In native English homes, as in other cultures, parenting may be varied. In many homes women may take the lead role, but this is not a universal truth! The concept of culture cannot be considered without thinking about gender, wealth and status. The entry on *Equal opportunities* offers further guidance.

Cultural differences can conflict and confuse teachers who have one set of expectations that are challenged by children who come from different backgrounds. Most people have ideas about their own identity. English nationals who are teachers, on the whole, are middle-class, white and, in primary schools, female; because of this middle-class culture may be predominant in the schools where they teach. The community culture may be quite different. Where the community culture is different to their own background, teachers may have lower expectations about academic achievement. The children you teach and their parents have ideas about how you will behave and what to expect from you. These ideas can be brought into school and may be challenging to deal with.

Further reading

See the equal opportunities reading list.
On the web the British Council site is a helpful starting place for finding out about culture in other countries www.britcoun.org
Embassy sites are often helpful as well www.ukwebstart.com or www2. tagish.co.uk/links/embassy are both useful links.

TAA Standards

1.1, 1.2, 2.4, 3.3.6.

Curriculum

Legal and prescribed curricula vary from country to country. Some countries, such as England, have a very prescribed curriculum with a detailed syllabus for each subject (Programmes of Study) and clear sets of criterion referenced levels of achievement (Attainment Targets). This is strongly monitored through national testing (SATs) and inspection (Ofsted). Published league tables of school results for 11-year-olds ensure that schools are in competition with themselves and other local schools. In contrast, some developing countries struggle to ensure that their populations gain basic literacy.

Whatever approach your country/state takes, there will be legal requirements and maybe highly recommended guidance, such as the National Literacy and Numeracy Strategies (England). Countries/

states will have ways of monitoring the system and will have expectations about raising the achievement of pupils.

Long- and medium-term plans should provide a balance of subjects across the year with opportunities to review and develop understanding. If a school has long-term plans in place these will have taken into account the legal requirements of delivery. Some curricula have built-in opportunities to revisit topics. This is sometimes referred to as the 'spiral curriculum'. In most countries, the style of teaching is left to the teacher. This is because it is recognized that each teacher will find particular styles more effective for them than others.

Links

Culture
Equal opportunities
Ethnicity
Long-term planning
Medium-term planning
Standardized tests
Summative assessment

Strategies

- At an initial planning stage, check that it will be possible to cover the required curriculum throughout the year.
- Indicate, at one of the levels of planning, references to required documentation.
- Plan so the children get a variety of experiences.
- If possible, link topics across subjects.
- Allow time for assessment activities.
- Allow children opportunities to apply knowledge as well as to acquire it.

Development

Establishing curricula is a controversial issue. On the one hand, a detailed syllabus ensures that every child has an entitlement to a particular body of knowledge and skills. What that body of knowledge and skills should be is always going to be in debate. What controls are there on what goes in the curriculum? That rather depends on what you consider is the purpose of education and how you achieve that purpose. Society and groups within society have different expectations about education. There will always be religious, cultural and political tensions. One might ask what expectations parents and pupils have of education? Barrow (2001) debates the tension between a pure knowledge-based curriculum and one controlled by more pragmatic needs.

Another aspect of the curriculum which is evolving is the balance between teaching and assessment. In England assessment has dramatically increased within the last few years. Whilst this puts pressure on teachers to deliver the prescribed curriculum, does it improve learning? Does the learning improve over a narrower range of topics? Is this appropriate? As you see, lots of questions for debate.

From a social perspective a lot more goes on in school than delivery of academic subjects. Some have termed this 'the hidden curriculum'. This covers all those social and life skills that pupils acquire by being with other pupils. For some, this is the main attraction of coming to school and matters far more to them than the formal learning.

The structure of the National Curriculum in England

From the age of 5 until the age of 14 all children are taught English, mathematics, science, geography, design and technology, information and communications technology (ICT), art, music, history, religious education and physical education. When they enter secondary education at the age of 11 the subjects also include a modern foreign language and citizenship. After the age of 14 the number of compulsory subjects is reduced, students can 'drop' history, geography, and art and design and music. (Subjects included in the National Curriculum can and do change so check the DfES websites for the most up-to-date information. A useful place to start is on Teachernet, www.teachernet.gov.uk, which gives links to other sites.)

The 14–19 curriculum allows for some variations in its approach to learning. Students may follow a traditional academic route in school and college. Some may take vocational or occupational subjects, which will include work-based learning.

The National Curriculum is only part of a school's curriculum. It is also expected that children will use the core subjects of English, maths, science and ICT across the curriculum. In England and Wales, all children follow a Religious Education syllabus, usually locally agreed between various faith groups. Schools are expected to have a daily act of collective worship. Teachers take some responsibility for children's general welfare, health education, including sex and drugs education, and deal with more general issues outside the narrowly defined National Curriculum, such as sustainable development and environmental education. In England, all secondary schools are expected to include Key and Core Skills teaching across all subjects.

The National Curriculum is divided into four Key Stages:

Key Stage 1 is for children aged 5–7, Years 1 and 2.
Key Stage 2 is for 7–11-year-olds, Years 3–6.
Key Stage 3 is for 12–14-year-olds, Years 7–9.
Key Stage 4 is for 14–16-year-olds Years 10–11.

In England many children enter school nursery classes at the age of 3. They follow a foundation stage curriculum until they leave reception. This is called Key Stage Foundation. The 16–19 curriculum can be called Key Stage 5.

Each subject in the English National Curriculum has a programme of study. This sets out what should be taught in each stage and each year group. The attainment targets and level descriptions are also set out on a subject by subject basis. There are eight levels for all subjects, except for citizenship. There is also a description for exceptional performance beyond level 8. Each level describes what children are able to do. At the end of each Key Stage there are national tests and teacher assessment.

Key Stage 1 levels are 1–3, with most children at age 7 expected to achieve level 2.
Key Stage 2 levels are 2–5, with most children at age 11 expected to achieve level 4.
Key Stage 3 levels are 3–7, with most children at age 14 expected to achieve level 5/6.

In England, most Key Stage 3 students are assessed at the age of 14 on National Curriculum tests in reading, writing (including handwriting), spelling, mathematics, mental arithmetic and science. They are assessed by teachers in all subjects. These tests and assessments take place in May each year. The results are published for each school so that comparisons can be made. Some adjustments to results are made, based on things such as entitlement to free school meals, which allows for schools to be compared.

At Key Stage 4 subjects are mainly assessed through national qualifications. Schools' results are publicly reported for account-ability purposes on the number of grade C or better that their students achieve at GCSE.

Students enter secondary school having followed the Key Stage 2 curriculum. The information about each student's achievement is passed on from school to school.

Further reading

Barrow, R. (2001) 'Knowledge and the curriculum' in Pollard, A. (Ed.) *Readings for Reflective Teaching in the Primary School*, London: Continuum.

Dearing, R. (1993) *The National Curriculum and its Assessment: a Review*, London: Schools Curriculum and Assessment Authority (SCAA).

Department for Education and Employment (DfEE) (1998) *The National Literacy Strategy*, London: DfEE.

Department for Education and Employment (DfEE) (1999) *The National Numeracy Strategy*, London: DfEE.

Department for Education and Employment (DfEE) (2000) *The National Curriculum: Handbook for Primary Teachers in England Key Stages 1 and 2*, London: DfEE/QCA (http://www.nc.uk.net).

Hughes, P. (2000) *Principles of Primary Education – Study Guide*, London: David Fulton.

Moyles, J. and Robinson, G. (Eds) (2002) *Beginning Teaching: Beginning Learning in Primary Education*, 2nd edn, Buckingham: Open University Press.

TTA Standards

2.2, 2.3.

Demonstration by the teacher

Demonstrating and explaining are both highly skilled forms of teaching. Having established your learning outcome, what it is the children are going to learn, you'll need to break down the demonstration into carefully considered steps. It helps to rehearse before working in front of the class.

Showing your class how to do something can be a highly effective teaching approach. Some procedures and skills are most effectively taught this way. Examples include showing children how to set out written work (margins, date, where to put their name, what to do about corrections etc.) and safe ways of carrying equipment. You need to teach children precisely how you want these things done. Then they need opportunity to practise the procedure or skill. You need to check that things are as they should be. You'll probably need to remind and correct them fairly frequently to start with. Eventually procedures and skills become automatic. However, remember that a procedure or skill learnt in one environment, or under one condition, will not necessarily transfer to new situations. For instance, safety rules learned in science will need to be demonstrated and taught again in craft lessons. This is concrete and holistic teaching. Children see what it is you do and then they can replicate it.

Demonstration through telling and using examples to model thinking is another highly effective teaching approach. For example, in mathematics a teacher might get at a general statement through careful questions and appropriate examples discussed in depth. Or, in English and social science subjects, to create informed opinion the teacher may argue aloud, putting forward various points of view and the reasons why some are more convincing than others. Examples need to be carefully considered. Case studies worked through in pairs and groups, with children explaining the work and their thinking about it to each other and to the teacher, can be very useful. The work often needs to be placed in a sequence of practice, review and then application to new situations.

Links

Active learning
Communicating clearly
Communication about learning
Independent learning
Instruction
Learning styles
Pace
Safety
Skills and strategies
Whole class teaching

Strategies

Before you start:

- Make sure that you have everything you need for the demonstration.

- Make sure you are absolutely accurate in the demonstration.
- Think carefully about pace; be slow enough to be clear, but not so slow that it's boring.
- Make sure you've thought about safety.
- Practise your demonstration – rehearse your questions, predict possible answers, think about what might go wrong and what you'll do to put things right.

In class:

- Move children so that everyone can clearly see what it is you are demonstrating.
- Tell them exactly what it is that is being demonstrated.
- 'Think aloud', modelling the procedure, skill and thinking.
- Use carefully chosen questions.
- Listen and respond to answers.
- When appropriate get children to predict what might happen.
- Have some poor examples for children to critique.
- Do some examples steps by step.
- If you are demonstrating a way of thinking, make the 'laws' of the subject explicit.
- If you are demonstrating a way of thinking, use case studies to show how ideas are used in practice.
- Give opportunities to practise with your support.
- Teach children how to check for themselves.
- Be prepared to re-teach until everyone has understood and can do what is required.

Development

Much of your teaching will be demonstration, so it's worth thinking about what makes it effective for the learner. Sousa (2001) reminds us that the brain responds positively to humour, movement, using all the senses – touch, smell, feel as well as listening. Humour for example, has physiological benefits in that it wakes the brain up and, used with care, it is an attention grabber. It helps to create a positive environment for learning and it helps people to remember.

Further reading

Cowley, S. (1999) *Starting Teaching: How to Succeed and Survive*, London: Continuum.

Hughes, P. (2000) *Principles of Primary Education – Study Guide*, London: David Fulton.

Sousa, D. A. (2001) *How the Brain Learns*, 2nd edn, Thousand Oaks: Corwin.

Differentiation

All groups of pupils have a range of ability and needs. As a student teacher or a new teacher to the school, collecting information about pupils' needs and abilities begins on preliminary visits. Through observation, questioning and listening to pupils, talking to the teacher and looking at records you should be able to acquire sufficient information to plan detailed schemes. At first you will plan work which you think is appropriate for a particular group of pupils, but as you get to know them and you observe their responses, you will be able to plan the next piece of work so that it more closely matches what they need. This will probably involve modifying your medium-term planning as you go along. Remember, your planning needs to include consideration of gender, culture and race as well as academic performance.

You can differentiate your teaching in three ways:

1. by task;
2. by outcome;
3. by support.

Some tasks can be given to all the pupils and they will be able to respond and learn from them. The task allows them to respond at their own level, this is called differentiation by outcome. Other tasks will only benefit certain groups, therefore different tasks or variations of the original task are given to each group. This is called differentiation by task.

When you differentiate by support you will be responding to individual needs. This could involve helping individuals, but also adapting goals as you work with the children. For example, when you see that an able child has clearly understood the work set, you might reduce the practice task and set him/her a more challenging task where he/she has to apply the information. If another child is struggling you might simplify the task or give a task which underpins the one he/she is attempting.

By differentiating tasks you are trying to facilitate learning. By matching the task to the children's ability you are enabling them to build on prior knowledge and move forward. If the task is well matched, the child will engage in the task and learn from doing it.

Links

Able children
Active learning
Formative assessment
Group work
Independent learning
Questioning
Special Educational Needs
Whole class teaching

Strategies

- Collect information about level of performance and past experience prior to medium-term planning.
- Select grouping appropriate to the learning objective. (If all the pupils cannot respond, differentiation needs to occur).
- Make minor adjustments to objectives, if necessary, as you work with the children. (This involves having thought about possible extensions and simplifications when planning the lesson.)

Development

Whilst everyone recognizes that children learn at different paces and there is a range of ability in every age group, there is little agreement as how best to cater for the range. This is probably because there is no solution which is entirely obvious. Some primary schools run mixed ability classes throughout the timetable, some schools set for certain subjects such as mathematics, and some schools set the children for the whole timetable (sometimes called streaming). Even within mixed ability classes some grouping will probably take place, either all the time or partially with different groups for different subjects. There is a trend recently to do more whole class teaching. This does not mean that pupils' different needs go away, they are catered for in a different way, such as various levels of teachers' questions and expectations of different pupil outputs.

There is evidence that placing children in ability groups has an effect on learning and self-esteem. Brophy and Good (1970) found that there was a sequence of low self-esteem and low teacher expectation generated by grouping students in ability groups, which contributed to low performance. Boaler *et al.* (2000) have explored students' perceptions at secondary school level and raised some thoughtful issues that are well worth considering. Setting in primary schools in mathematics, in the United Kingdom, has increased since the 1980s, ostensibly to meet the demands of the new curriculum. This research was carried out with 13- and 14-year-olds moving from mixed ability to sets in mathematics. They found little evidence that students felt that they were in a better learning environment. The results indicated that the lower sets generated low student self-esteem and low expectation from teachers. This was poorly justified by a very small percentage of able children who coped with the speed of work in the top set. Teachers tended not to differentiate within lessons and a whole class teaching model dominated in set situations. Many children appeared to find the single pace difficult to respond to.

Further reading

Boaler, J., Wiliam, D. and Brown, M. (2000) 'Students' experience of ability grouping – disaffection, polarisation and the construction of failure', *British Educational Research Journal*, 26: 5, 631–48.

Brophy, J. and Good, T. (1970) 'Teachers' communication of differential expectations for children's classroom performance: some behavioural data', *Journal of Educational Psychology*, 61, 365–74.

TTA Standards

3.3.4, 3.3.6.

Discipline

Discipline helps children behave acceptably in school. Discipline is intended to repress and redirect misbehaviour. Over time, the goal is to reduce the need for teacher intervention so that children learn to control themselves. Discipline is about the ways that children behave towards each other and to their teachers and the ways that teachers behave towards children. The rules that will be implemented must take account of the needs of the whole child, the needs of society and for good order in the school.

The school behaviour policy establishes what it is that teachers do about discipline. The values held by school staff and implemented in the behaviour policy may conflict with those held by the parents. This means that children may find that behaviour accepted at home has to be modified for school. Establishing a common set of values is never going to be easy. Teachers and the other adults in school may not agree with each other about what is acceptable behaviour. Time and effort has to be made to work through to an agreed set of values to underpin the school behaviour policy. Schools that tackle this through involving the children, parents and the community often develop very successful policies. School becomes the place where the child is made aware of and learns to deal with the similarities and differences between the values that occur at home, at school, in the street and, eventually, at work.

Links

Bullying
Culture
Emotional development
Equal opportunities
Ethnicity
Inclusion
Relationships with pupils
Safety
Special Educational Needs
Values and ethos
Working with adults

Strategies

I will implement school rules fairly by:

- having high expectations:
    setting high standards of behaviour e.g. treating children politely by using their names and a pleasant but firm tone of voice; through carefully teaching the rules e.g. that 'sit down, thank-you' means put your bottom on your chair and your two feet and the four chair legs on the floor, that turn-taking means listening and responding, not everyone talking at once;
- being aware of the needs of the children and taking account of their age and experience
    e.g. by knowing that not all children find conforming to the rules easy, by knowing who these children are and increasing the

behaviour demands in small steps and rewarding even the smallest improvement;

e.g. by being aware that school rules and the way I interpret them may severely conflict with the home rules or lack of rule, realizing that the match between the child's expectations and mine may need to be negotiated, allowing time for the child to come to terms and deal with this conflict;

- developing children's understanding of the need for safety and security and risk in their own development, thus increasing their ability to be independent learners and moving them towards autonomy by, for example, offering choice; in activities, in making decisions about classroom routines and in selecting appropriate rewards and punishments;
- knowing about cultural, racial differences and expectations, treating these differences respectfully and using this knowledge to reward and punish appropriately;
- developing the child's moral and social understanding:
  recognizing that the classroom is one place where social understanding can be developed by raising and dealing with issues, for example, moral dilemmas such as 'when is it right to tell?' through discussion and group work.

Development

Misbehaviour is behaviour considered to be inappropriate in the context in which it occurs. In school this will include:

aggression – both physical and verbal and including bullying;
immorality – lying, cheating stealing;
defiance;
class disruption – where children talk out of turn or hinder each other;
being off task – day dreaming, text messaging, the American expression is *goofing off*.

The last two, whilst minor in themselves, constitute the most frequent interruptions to teaching and learning. Many school behaviour policies put considerable emphasis on reducing disruptions and off-task behaviour through carefully managing the teaching and learning in classrooms. The first three may be addressed in a number of ways. For example, reducing opportunities for bullying by having 'befrienders', children trained to look after those who find the playground difficult.

Teachers use techniques such as 'circle time' to work on developing a strong class ethos in which pupils are empowered to, for example:

> deal with issues of right and wrong;
> decide what is and what is not acceptable behaviour;
> discuss what working well means;
> explore how to resist peer pressure;
> address current moral issues.

Punishment for failing to keep to rules also has to be considered. Punishment has to be just and must not deny the child access to the curriculum. The really serious 'telling off', by you or a more senior teacher can be effective. The telling off has a number of steps, these may include:

> Identification of the misdemeanour (what the child did, e.g. 'The rule in our school is that we treat each other well, in the playground, you hit John, that breaks our rule').
> The consequences of the child's action in breaking the rules ('John was hit and that hurt him, he has a bruise').
> Getting the child to acknowledge that the rule was broken ('Did you know that Mrs Smith saw you hit John?'. Use other sources of evidence if you meet resistance.)
> A set of actions for preventing repetition agreed with the child.

The loss of privilege can be effective. The point is to keep focused on what the child did, 'you are being punished for breaking our rule', not because 'you're bad'.

To be successful, the child must regard the punishment awarded as fair. A way must be offered to enable the child to learn to avoid repeating the offence.

Further reading

All these books offer excellent introductions on how to achieve good order and discipline in school.

Cowley, S. (2001) *Getting the Buggers to Behave*, London: Continuum.
Mosely, J. (1999) *More Quality Circle Time*, Cambridge: LDA.
Mosely, J. (1996) *Quality Circle Time*, Cambridge: LDA.

Rodgers, B. (2000) *Behaviour Management: A Whole School Approach*, London: Paul Chapman.

Thody, A., Gray, B. and Bowden, D. (2000) *The Teacher's Survival Guide*, London: Continuum.

TTA Standards
2.7, 3.2.4, 3.3.9.

Displays

Displays can be informative, rewarding or interactive. A teacher may decide to put up a display as a stimulus for a new topic. This raises the children's awareness of what is to come and gives them time to seek out contributions. Children, like adults, also like to know the programme ahead of the event, especially if they are required to contribute. Children like to see their own work on display. This is rewarding and motivating for them. The purpose of interactive displays is to allow learning to take place through children taking some action prompted by the display. The children visit the site and manipulate the materials physically or mentally, e.g. by answering the questions posed. This offers an opportunity for reinforcement of something that has taken place in a lesson, or an opportunity to extend learning on a topic therefore this type of display is particularly useful at either end of the ability range. Examples of such a display might be sorting shapes, interpreting graphs, making circuits, setting the table, interpreting maps, the role-play corner or a computer program. The advantages of the interactive display are that the children can work at their own pace and the teacher can be elsewhere in the classroom.

All displays should be well presented. If there is sufficient paper, double mounting helps to show work at its best. Neat titles and labelling with vertical and horizontal alignment give a professional look. Sometimes a few items look better than a crowded board. Changes in texture and pattern on the background add variety and depth to the overall look.

Links
Purposeful working atmosphere

Strategies

- Use a variety of types of display, interactive, stimulus, quality completed work.
- In medium-term planning identify lessons which will generate display materials.
- In medium-term planning decide which topics could be supported by an interactive display.
- In medium-term planning identify the resources you need to acquire, in time for you to find them.
- If a lesson is going to provide display material, plan an appropriate pupil output.
- Over several weeks, ensure that each child has a piece of quality work displayed.
- Double mount work where appropriate.
- Plan the layout of the display, use pins to arrange it before stapling, gluing or blue-tacking.
- Label clearly so that visitors to your room understand what the display is about.

Early Learning Goals

The Early Learning Goals are the expected outcomes of the Foundation Stage (3–5 years) in England. These goals span nursery and reception class provision and children are expected to be working towards them in any educational establishment that is inspected. There are six areas of learning to be developed:

1. personal, social and emotional development;
2. communication, language and literacy;
3. mathematics;
4. knowledge and understanding of the world;
5. physical development;
6. creative development.

In the document *Curriculum Guidance for the Foundation Stage* (DfES, 2000) the Early Learning Goals are given and suggestions for progression through early years' education towards achieving them. This guidance is referred to as 'Stepping Stones' and offers activity suggestions at three levels of difficulty.

Links

Baseline assessment
Curriculum
Emotional development
Formative assessment
Intellectual development
Linguistic development
Long-term planning
Medium-term planning
Play and structured learning
Social development

Strategies

- Plan to visit areas of development several times through the year (long-term planning).
- Provide for a range of experiences within the areas of development (medium-term planning).
- Track individual development within the goals (formative assessment).
- Provide experiences where gaps are perceived from your record keeping.

Development

Some would argue that a curriculum should not be imposed on pre-school children, no matter how open and exciting it might be. The danger of providing a curriculum is that schools and teachers have different interpretations of what is required in styles of delivery. It would be easy to attempt to formalize the curriculum and expect children to behave as older pupils. This is not what is intended. Whilst there is a slight feeling of a 'top down' model, the guidance and goals set out to give young children an entitlement of experience. The fact that only certain provision (that which is inspected) is expected to address this curriculum, means that not all children are going to get the same provision. The fact that no child has to attend school until the term in which they are 5 years old (England) adds to the unevenness of provision. Further, there is a significant number of providers of early years' education who believe that free play is the mode of operation for the child in the early years. Ensuring consistent provision towards achievement of the Early Learning Goals would be challenging in this scenario.

Further reading

Department for Education and Skills (DfES) (2000) *Curriculum Guidance for the Foundation Stage*, London: DfEE/QCA.

Emotional development

Being able to make judgements about another's feelings, the emotional state, develops from birth. Judgements about emotion are made on the continuum of happiness to sadness; the emotions of fear, anger, rage, guilt and shame. Through childhood into early adolescence an ability to understand how others feel becomes increasingly sophisticated. As the child's intellectual understanding develops, it seems that more than one emotion and the relationship between them becomes established, e.g. by 8 years old many children will say things like, 'I'm cross when I'm interrupted, but I'm happy to go out to play'.

Babies connect first with those who care for them. Adults are able to reinforce the expressions that their 6–8 week old babies make. Smiles are met with smiles; facial expressions are used to monitor the supposed emotion. This seems to be the beginning of developing a range of emotions. The baby's smiles are gradually given more readily to the adults who make most difference to him/her. 7–9 month old babies show 'stranger distress' (Sroufe, 1996); the emotions of fear and anger also develop at about this time. Much of the display of emotion seems to be part of intellectual growth. There seems no doubt that toddlers learn, from the reactions of others, a whole range of emotions and how to show these. For example, by age 2, infants will switch from pouting to crying if this is to their advantage.

Children move, over time, from having others help them control their emotions, to being more able to do this for themselves. Some researchers suggest that emotional regulation goes on throughout our life span (Thompson, 1991). Individuals vary hugely in the amount of self-regulation displayed. Think how easily some people cry, whilst others seem unable to show any emotions.

There are two areas of study that are associated with our understanding of emotion. One is temperament. You'll know the sort of person that you are, for example you might 'be able to argue for England', or you might be easy going, taking everything in your stride. Your temperament is closely tied to your emotional type. The other area of study is the work on attachment between babies and parents. Early nurturing and differences in child care may make a difference to emotional development. These two aspects begin to explain why children may react differently in the classroom contexts.

Links

Intellectual development
Linguistic development
Social development

Further reading

Keenan, T. (2002) *An Introduction to Child Development*, London: Sage.
Sroufe, L. A. (1996) *Emotional Development: The Organization of Emotional Life in the Early Years*, New York: Wiley.
Thompson, R. A. (1991) 'Emotional regulation and emotional development', *Educational Psychology Review*, 3: 269–307.

TAA Standards

1.2, 2.4.

English as an additional language

English as an additional language (EAL) is an everyday experience in many classrooms. In England, 'over half a million children do not have English as a first language' (DfEE, 1997: 34). Every teacher is expected to promote EAL in their teaching. The question is, does spoken and written language and reading develop 'naturally' or does something have to be done about it in school? Often the natural approach works quite well, especially for very young children who may seem to learn easily and rapidly. After they are about 8 years old some bilingual children seem not to progress as well as others. It appears that there may be a barrier to achieving in school if we leave the teaching of English to chance. Many schools have a specific policy, curriculum and staff with expertise for success in EAL which you will need to use.

Links

Culture
Equal opportunities

Ethnicity
Linguistic development

Strategies

First, establish some facts:

- What country and language(s)?
- Refugee or migrant? (Think of culture shock for both, think of additional stresses of being a refugee.)
- How much English is spoken at home?
- Are there other children or adults in school with the same language?

Then do what you can to promote and maintain the child's first language:

- Find someone who speaks the child's language.
- Continue the learning in the child's own language as much and for as long as possible.
- Remember listening (getting the child to hear English) precedes talking and speech precedes reading and writing.
- It is also worth reminding yourself that the conventions of English, where we read from left to right and the writing 'sits' on the line, may be very different to the child's own language.

Development

Many children who are learning EAL grow up to be fluent and literate in English. They may also speak their first language well but not always read or write it. If we insist that children only speak English we are making a statement about the value we place on homes and families. The child's heritage needs to be valued. The language of the home and the community need to be celebrated. Ideally, we might want to promote bilingualism or even multilingualism. This means that whilst we expect children to use English for communication both in spoken and written form, and to know about its rules, grammar and conventions; we would at the same time, be actively promoting the child's first and additional languages. This is a cross curricular, cross phase challenge. Children with EAL offer a remarkable enrichment to the life of a school.

Further reading

DfEE (1997) *Excellence in Schools*, London: Stationery Office.
Mohan, B., Leung, C. and Davidson, C. (Eds) (2001) *English as a Second Language in the Mainstream: Teaching, Learning and Identity*, London: Longman.

TTA Standards

3.2.5, 3.3.5.

Equal opportunities

A useful place to start is to think about who we are and what contributes to our values. This list is not comprehensive, but think about:

your *gender* including sexual orientation;
what you look like, your *physical appearance*, things like race, disability, age;
the sort of *family* you come from, nuclear, extended, single parent ... ;
your *religion* and *culture*;
your ability to *communicate*, including your language, standard English dialect, Yorkshire dialect, English as an additional language ... ;
where you *live*, inner city, suburbs, in the country ... ;
and, perhaps most importantly, your *wealth* or *status*, i.e. middle income, low income, professional job, clerical job, unskilled job.

Some of these, maybe all of them, will contribute to your identity. Teaching is not a neutral activity, so your values and who you are, will have an effect on those whom you teach. Equal opportunities is about being inclusive in the way you deal with all pupils. Treating all children the same will not serve. To be fair you have to meet the needs of individuals as far as you can. Children's attitudes to school come from their home and their community. Often these might conflict with teachers' norms. Your expectations and theirs may not match. Their experience of things like the way you talk might be unfamiliar. When you ask once, at home they may be nagged. What you say as a joke may be misunderstood, regarded as offensive or even as racist. In your teaching, help all children to:

76

ıemselves;

ımilarities between their own lives and the lives of others;

n from each other;

ɔt feel that they are better than others because of their race, gender or wealth.

Links

Culture

English as an additional language

Ethnicity

Expectations about pupils' learning

Gender

Inclusion

Resources

Rewards

Strategies

Create an inclusive classroom in which:

- You are conscious that your own attitudes are influential by, for example,

  making a real effort to get unfamiliar names correct;

  valuing the process of learning as well as the product;

  avoiding remarks that start, 'girls don't . . .', 'boys don't . . .';

  setting high expectations about success.

- Children's home experience is valued by, for example, building a partnership with parents which enables you to emphasize the similarities and positive aspects of different families' life at home.

- You deal with questions about gender, race, and disability frankly and honestly, for example:

  getting children to describe how they look using facts, eye colour, skin colour, body parts.

- You deal with any name calling sensitively:

  support the victim;

  encourage other ways of dealing with feelings through, for example, circle time;

  reference to school policy.

- Adult to adult relationships in school provide positive role-models for children, for example, by distribution of roles that avoids gender bias.

University of Chichester

Item Title	Due Date
* Understanding maths : basic mathematics explained	16/10/2020
* How children learn	16/10/2020
* Equality and education	16/10/2020
* Introduction to education studies	25/09/2020
* How to be a brilliant trainee teacher	16/10/2020
* teacher's guide to classroom research	25/09/2020
* Improving Primary Mathematics Teaching and Learning.	25/09/2020
* primary teacher's handbook	16/10/2020

* Indicates items borrowed today

www.intellident.co.uk
email support@intellident.co.uk

- Your teaching is planned and delivered with equality of opportunity always considered. Plan to:

  use children's prior experience;

  use collaborative group work;

  ensure that girls, minority ethnic children and boys all get to take leading roles;

  differentiate tasks;

  allow for same-sex paired work;

  allow for first language to be used in pair work;

  choose resources that are checked for bias, use positive images and are up-to-date.

- In predominantly white schools ensure that the curriculum reflects a multi-racial society.

Development

This is a complex area and one where it is easy to feel 'in the wrong'. At a personal level it often seems too hard to be fair to all the children in the class all the time. Some children do need more of your attention and time at particular points. If you feel this is happening too often, you should do something about it. One way is to consciously limit yourself to spending slightly less time with more demanding children and slightly more time with those who less often get your full attention.

Further reading

Cole, M., Hill, D. and Shan, S. (Eds) (1997) *Promoting Equality in Primary Schools*, London: Cassell. One of the most comprehensive textbooks around, this deal's both with the theoretical background and the practical outcomes for teachers.

Mosely, J. (1999) *More Quality Circle Time*, Cambridge: LDA.

Mosely, J. (1996) *Quality Circle Time*, Cambridge: LDA.

Two practical books which provide a sound way of dealing with many sensitive issues.

Shilela, A. (2002) 'Dialogue with a difference: teaching for equality in primary schools', in Moyles, J. and Robinson, G. (Eds) *Beginning Teaching: Beginning Learning in Primary Education*, 2nd edn, Buckingham: Open University.

There are very good sources on the WWW.

www.cre.gov.uk has good links to many educational resources.

www.dfes.gov.uk is the place to look for up-to-date central government guidance.

TTA Standard

3.3.14.

Ethnicity

In the UK population of approximately 54 million about 6 per cent
are from minority ethnic groups, (1991 census figures). Ballard and
Kalra, (1994, p. 11) estimate that about 11 per cent of the school
population are from minority ethnic groups. The drive from the
UK government is to ensure that all children in our schools achieve
high standards. In the past there is evidence that some groups, for
example both Afro-Caribbean pupils (Gillborn and Mirza, 2000) and
white boys from working-class background are doing less well in
public examinations and national tests. For teachers in England,
developing an understanding and having a positive attitude about
children from different ethnic backgrounds, along with a
commitment to their success is a requirement (Children Act, 1989)
as well as a professional standard (DfES/TTA, 2002). As a teacher you
will have a set of expectations about the children you teach. In part
this will result from your own ethnicity. Your race, like your status in
society and your gender, raises expectations in the children you
teach and from their parents. They will come to school with
attitudes informed by their families' experience in the community.
Home behaviour towards adults may be very different from your
own. Your awareness about other ethnic groups will inform your
teaching. Knowing about differences means that you can choose
methods, resources and examples that will help your learners. It
also helps to avoid misunderstandings and false expectations.

Links

Culture
Equal opportunities
Gender

Strategies

See strategies suggested for *Equal opportunities.*

Development

Cole (1997, p. 53) argues that in UK schools there are three
approaches to education and that each is a strongly held position.

Some schools have a monocultural attitude that, 'attempts to make everyone "socially and culturally British"'. Others adopt a multicultural policy that celebrates cultural and religious difference. The last group adopts anti-racist policies that actively challenges all aspects of discrimination. Any of the above positions seem to place schooling as central in attitude forming. This would suggest that what teachers do about this issue is important.

Further reading

Ballard, R. and Kalra, V. S. (1994) *Ethnic Dimensions of the 1991 Census: A Preliminary Report*, Manchester: University of Manchester Census Group.

Cole, M., Hill, D. and Shan, S. (Eds) (1997) *Promoting Equality in Primary Schools*, London: Cassell.

Cole, M. (1997) 'Equality and Primary Education: What are the conceptual issues?', in Cole, M., Hill, D. and Shan, S. (Eds) *Promoting Equality in Primary Schools*, London: Cassell, pp. 48–75.

Department for Education and Skills/Teacher Training Agency (2002) *Qualifying to Teach, Professional Standards for Qualified Teacher Status and Requirements for Initial Teacher Training*, TPU 0803/02-02, London: TTA, (weblink www.canteach.gov.uk).

Gillborn, D. and Mirza, H. S. (2000) *Educational Inequality: Mapping Race, Class and Gender; A Synthesis of Research Evidence*, London: Ofsted, see website www.ofsted.gov.uk

TTA Standards

3.1.2, 3.3.6.

Evaluating lessons (assessing the meeting of learning objectives)

Lessons are evaluated for several reasons. The main one is to ensure learning has taken place. You will need to assess whether the children have met the set objective(s). If they have this will inform you that the lesson was effective and will provide information for individual records. When learning has not taken place it is important to reflect on what has happened and make decisions about adjusting the approach. It might be that the objective was not appropriate for all or some of the children. Maybe it was too hard or too easy, and because of this the children did not engage in the work. It might be that the planned activities did not match and support the objective. Possibly they learned something else or were confused. Maybe your teaching techniques still need to be developed so that a purposeful working atmosphere can be created. Maybe a combination of snow-fall, dentist and school photographer has completely disrupted the lesson. In this case, even the best teachers give in gracefully.

Once you have analysed the lesson you need to make decisions about how you will approach the next lesson. Your decided action might be appropriate for all your lessons or a strategy you plan to use during the teaching of that particular subject or group.

Links
Active learning
Formative assessment
Independent learning
Learning objectives
Medium-term planning
Summative assessment
Target setting

Strategies
A simple evaluation of the lesson might fall into the following categories:

Children	Noted individual performance to records/who needs help.
Activity	Did the activities support the objectives well and would I use them again?
Teacher	What teacher skills did I use well/need to change?

Development
There are a lot of things which can go wrong with lessons. Even for the best teachers, lessons which go really well are not as common as people think. One aim is to ensure that all lessons are of a reasonable quality. With good preparation and a continuing proactive approach to improving your teaching skills this should come about.

Moyles (1995, 109–10) describes the reflective process of evaluating lessons and medium-term plans:

'What we are essentially assessing is to what extent the children (and you) have been able to:
reach the objectives set for them in planning;
develop appropriate attitudes and opinions;

reach high standards and offer quality outcomes;
deal with the rates at which they learn;
find out about their strengths and weaknesses;
understand what learning should take place next for children to progress;
know what activities or experiences should now be provided or repeated
and what differentiated experiences are needed for which children.

Further reading

Moyles, J. (1995) (Ed.) *Beginning Teaching: Beginning Learning in Primary Education*, Buckingham: Open University.

Expectations about pupils' learning (challenge)

Challenge is about engaging children in thinking and working on the borders of their knowledge. Educational experience is a mixture of challenge, routine and review. Challenging children gives them the opportunity to take risks, to apply knowledge, to adopt new understanding, to work in context and to experience the thrill of being discoverers. This last is a highly motivating and engaging feeling.

Consider that most of the adult world is about routine and challenge. We do need to educate children to sustain routine, meet challenge and deal with both. Also, remember that all children can be challenged at their own level. It is not just a target for able pupils.

Children like to know where they are so that they have some control over the day. They also enjoy revisiting because it reaffirms their belief that there are things they can do and be successful at. Games, stories and computer programs are good examples of revisiting situations. They also like challenge where they are required to draw on their knowledge to resolve unfamiliar situations.

Teachers like to present a range of situations too. There are the times when routine is strong and skills and knowledge are built in a formal way without having to set up new procedures, for example spelling, skill-building exercises, diary writing. Then there are times when the teacher wants children to use the knowledge and skills they have acquired. This could be by asking children to bring their problem-solving skills to new situations which will lead to new learning or a chance to apply knowledge to a problem in a context they have already worked on.

Links

Able children

Active learning
Curriculum
Differentiation
Independent learning
Motivation
Problem solving
Thinking skills

Strategies

- Provide a balance through the week of the type of work provided; routine, new learning, review/consolidation, challenge.
- Ensure children have the opportunity to apply their knowledge in new contexts.
- Differentiate work where possible.
- Have lots of problem solving!

Development

There is a considerable body of evidence building, from the time of Piaget through to present day research into thinking skills, that problem solving contributes to developing effective learning skills. Challenging a person's thinking is what forces them to adjust or confirm the views that they already hold. Discussing how to solve problems means that a person has to articulate their ideas and have others comment on them. This is a strong strategy for clarifying and remembering. Maybe this is the territory where learning, which may be transferred to other new situations, takes place.

On a more individual note, it is worth reflecting on what our expectations are of particular children. Is it wise to form the view that they cannot possibly solve problems, that they are only capable of copying, that they can only manage book 4, that they need to work in this maths group because they are of low ability in language skills? Our perceptions of children are clearly conveyed by our communications with them. If we have low expectations, children will believe that is all they are capable of. We need to be very careful about what we convey and expect.

TTA Standards

3.1.1, 3.2.4.

Expectations of pupils' behaviour

See *Discipline.*

Explaining

Teaching by explanation is an effective way of encouraging learning. Poor explanation will be a source of frustration and tension in class. Careful preparation is a key to engaging pupils. Getting the right mixture of instruction, questioning and the pace of your whole class teaching is important. If children have not understood, you need to act. You could go over the explanation with the whole class, or with groups, or with individuals. If this happens often, you will need to alter the way you explain. Children, who need you to go over what you have just explained to the whole class, just for them, can be time consuming. Think about the additional explanation that these pupils will need and how you can plan this into the session. You may be able to use classroom assistants to do this or you may need to set the class going on activities and return afterwards to these pupils.

Links

Communicating clearly
Instruction
Pace
Questioning
Whole class teaching
Working with other adults

Strategies

- Make sure that you understand what you are explaining.
- Teach new material as soon as you have pupils' attention in a lesson.
- Make good use of any additional adults to support children who are unclear about what they are to do, or are slow at starting tasks.
- Take account of pupils' previous knowledge and experience of the topic.
- Link your explanation to pupils' knowledge, experience and interests.
- Use language that your pupils can understand.
- Tell pupils what it is that they are going to learn.
- Break your explanation into small steps.

- Use carefully chosen examples, have several different examples.
- Allow time for practice and rehearsal.
- Review your explanation with pupils at the end of the lesson.

Development

Sousa's (2001) analysis of a forty-minute lesson suggests that the first twenty minutes is the best time to introduce new information. He suggests that you should avoid asking pupils about the topic in the introduction to your explanation. This is because if you get a wrong answer from pupils at this point, it will 'contaminate' the explanation. The next ten to fifteen minutes should be used to allow pupils to engage on activities related to the new topic. The last chunk of time gives you a chance to review the new knowledge the pupils have. This is one style of teaching. Another school of thought would recommend a less formal approach where explanation follows challenge in the belief that the pupils develop a 'need to know' to resolve the situation. This can also lead to pupils explaining how things have been done.

Further reading

Sousa, D. A. (2001) *How the Brain Learns*, 2nd edn, Thousand Oaks: Corwin.

Wragg, E. C. and Brown, G. (1993) *Explaining*, London: Routledge. A very useful self-help text.

Feedback

Feedback is the provision of an evaluation on a piece of work or action. The feedback can be formal or informal and can come from a variety of sources. The usual person to provide feedback is the teacher, but there are occasions when appreciation is shown by others, such as:

parents at school assemblies or concerts, as a result of reading a school report;
the head teacher about good or bad work or behaviour;
other adults working in the classroom;
and peers.

As the teacher you will provide informal feedback as you respond in whole class, group and individual situations. Encouraging pupils' explanations about a task and the work they have done will help them to articulate their views. If you can then encourage pupils to suggest what action needs to be taken you are beginning to establish an approach to pupils' self-evaluation. Effective feedback should be constructive. It might begin with a critical view, but should end with the pupil being aware of how he/she can move forward.

Speaking on a one-to-one basis is probably the most effective feedback situation because you can have a dialogue with the pupil, but it is not always possible in the time available. Marking is a more traditional way of providing individual feedback. It is particularly useful when you have large classes and cannot speak to all individuals during the lesson time. It also allows you to respond to pupils from a distance (marking away from the classroom). Other forms of feedback include filling in competitive charts (e.g. spelling, learning tables, mental arithmetic, work cards) and rewards for competitive behaviour (e.g. smiley faces, house points, smarties in the jar). All these are extrinsic reward systems which assume the children appreciate the approval of others.

Pupils need to know how well they have done on tasks set. Feedback should be given promptly. All written work should be responded to. Helpful comments should be made to pupils on the way they have tackled tasks as well as on what they have achieved. All comments should be positive or constructive so that pupils can improve their response.

Links

Communication about learning
Competition
Marking
Motivation
Rewards
Thinking skills

Strategies

- Ensure feedback is given promptly.
- Offering constructive comments in whole class, group and individual situations.
- Through questioning, encourage pupils to explain their thinking and actions.
- Encourage pupils to decide what action needs to be taken.

- Setting up a reward system.
- Finding opportunities for others to reward with praise.
- Improve feedback within your marking system.

Development

Feedback, marking and reward are closely linked topics and need to be examined together, although one can be targeted whilst the others are maintained. In education, increasingly, value is being put on the quality and type of feedback. It is important that constructive feedback offers a balance to the increasing number of summative tests. Learning takes place more successfully when there is a dialogue between pupils and their teacher and between pupils and their peers. Talking about what they understand so far about a topic often clarifies issues. The opportunity to reflect on and rectify errors is tremendously important because pupils make errors at the limits of their learning and they need to establish correct understanding.

Smith (2001) suggests that if children give themselves feedback about the tasks that they are doing as they go along, then learning will be more established and connected in their brains. This feedback could be a parallel account of what is happening but it could be reflective, linked to previous experience or making hypotheses, each of which is a powerful support for learning.

Further reading

Smith, A. (2001) 'What the most recent brain research tells us about learning' in Banks, F. and Shelton Mayes, A. (Eds) *Early Professional Development for Teachers*, London: David Fulton/Open University.

TTA Standard

3.2.2.

Formative assessment (monitoring pupils' learning)

Most assessment in the classroom is formative, because teachers are trying to build on what children know, and to sort out misconceptions. Formative assessment occurs in several 'time frames'. From minute to minute you will be making decisions in the light of the pupils' responses, at the end of the lesson or day you will be assessing pupils' performance, your own teaching, and planning future action. Medium-term assessments and planning will also be part of the analysis which will feed into future planning.

A reasonable assessment expectation in an oral, whole class situation, is to note exceptionally good and exceptionally weak responses and get a general 'feel' for whole class understanding. When working orally with the whole class there are very few situations where it is possible to assess everyone's understanding. Group work or written responses provide a greater opportunity to observe or monitor pupils' performance. A group objective is a closer match to individual children's ability and therefore progress is expected and more likely to occur. In some lessons it is possible for the teacher to focus on a group and collect useful data.

It might be that the same learning objective(s) are visited in several lessons, so it is easier to build a picture of the class over a short period of time. Also, the objective is often returned to in the medium term in the form of assessments such as problems and tests.

A teacher may choose to assess what children know and can do prior to running a topic so that he/she can set more meaningful objectives in medium- and short-term planning.

Assessments can be formal, such as tests and exams, or informal such as talking and observing, but will be formative if you take action on the results. Formative assessments are a vital part of the cycle of effective teaching. They are used to inform your next planning and teaching as well as recording individual progress.

Links

Differentiation
Evaluating lessons
Feedback
Medium-term planning
Recording individual progress
Summative assessment
Target setting

Strategies

- Observe and question children, respond appropriately to their answers and level of understanding.
- Assess and act upon the learning that has and has not taken place in a lesson (recording and future planning).

- Select appropriate information to record informally and formally (consider purpose).
- Use formative assessment on your own teaching skills (self-evaluation).

Development

Assessment is used for many different purposes and therefore it is important that you select a form of assessment which provides you with the information you need. For a good summary of the purposes and principles of assessment refer to Harlen *et al.* in Pollard (1996) p. 264.

Further reading

Harlen, W., Gipps, C., Broadfoot, P. and Nuttall, D. (1996) 'Assessment purposes and principles' in Pollard, A. (Ed.) *Readings for Reflective Teaching in the Primary School*, London: Cassell.

TTA Standard

3.2.2.

Gender

Gender is as much about how we dress as it is about biological factors. To be seen as a man or a woman will be determined by the rules that a society has for these at a moment in time. Your experience of gender will be influenced by your up-bringing. It is also likely that your experience will be different to that experienced by those who brought you up. Your schooling, your friends and your experience of work all make your experience of being a man or a woman unique. In your teaching recognize that your uniqueness is both an advantage and a disadvantage. As a teacher you will have a set of expectations about the children you teach. Your gender, like your position in society and your race, raises expectations in the children you teach and in their parents. The differences in attitudes between you and them may be considerable. Some children have learned from the home to disregard women. Some have learned to disregard men. It should be noted that achievement for girls in the UK seems to be out-stripping that of boys at many stages. Your awareness about gender will inform your teaching as gender influences the way children behave and learn. Smith, (2001, p. 120) quoting work by Moir and Jessell (1993) has a useful summary of the differences. These include:

> boys are better at spatial reasoning, girls are better at language;
> girls talk before boys;
> boys talk and play more with inanimate objects;
> girls read character and social clues better;
> girls talk their way through maths problems, boys work non-verbally;
> girls are better at verbal activity, boys have better general maths ability;
> boys need more space than girls;
> boys have a shorter attention span.

These are, of course, generalizations. Many children will not conform to the stereotypes above. Nevertheless, knowing about these differences means that you can choose methods, resources and examples that will help your learners.

Links

Equal opportunities
Ethnicity
Learning styles
Research and its uses

Strategies

- Take account of gender differences in the way you teach.
- Use methods that stimulate both verbal and non-verbal learning.
- Use both visual aids and verbal instruction.
- Break learning into small steps, give opportunities to undertake whole tasks.
- Give tasks that demand an emotional response, role-play, discussion and debate, 'how would you feel if . . .'.
- Aim for a balance of activities that appeals to girls and to boys.
- Get children to challenge their preferred ways of learning by doing tasks that make them feel less comfortable.

Further reading

Cole, M., Hill, D. and Shan, S. (Eds) (1997) *Promoting Equality in Primary Schools*, London: Cassell.

Smith, A. (2001) 'The strategies that accelerate learning in the classroom', in Banks, F. and Shelton Mayes, A. (Eds) *Early Professional Development for Teachers*, London: Open University/David Fulton.

TTA Standard

3.3.14.

Group work

In many aspects of life we are required to work with others, so it is important that children learn how to co-operate with other children on tasks. Many school situations require individual learning and achievement and it is easy to overlook opportunities to work as a team and to work in different teams. It is interesting to see who takes the lead in group work, who has the ideas, who comes up with the solutions, who does the work leading to the presentation stage. With carefully structured groups, the teacher can foster these collaborative work skills. Problem solving is a good setting for group work, as is sport, drama and presentations.

Groups are often created in class to allow for differentiation of work. In this situation groups of like ability are placed together and provided with the same work. Even though they may be sitting round the same table, they may not be expected to work together. Mixed ability groups can also be used in appropriate situations. It is important for the teacher to decide which grouping is appropriate to the work which is to be done. Children's abilities may vary from subject to subject so there is a need to vary the way the groups are organized.

Links

Differentiation
Problem solving
Skills and strategies
Social development
Whole class teaching

Strategies

- Plan opportunities for group work in appropriate settings.
- Organize groups as well as allowing for free choice on occasions.

- Use ability groups when work needs to be differentiated.
- Vary the groups according to the tasks.

Development

Looking more closely at group work in the large ORACLE survey carried out in 1980 (Galton *et al.*) it was observed that children were mainly set individual tasks when sitting in groups, that most comments made between group members were managerial, only 9 per cent being intellectually stimulating exchanges.

McNamara (1996) visits some of the issues raised when ability groups are used, he comments that whole class teaching is a more effective learning strategy and finally suggests that the desks be arranged in a horseshoe shape for maximum attention and flexibility.

Bennett *et al.* (1984) in their research into classroom practice, observed a great deal of whole class teaching with the work aimed at the middle ability band with the set tasks being too easy or too difficult for half the pupils.

The social/academic benefits of legitimizing talk ought to help with establishing the task and in motivating children to complete their contribution, although sometimes the group dynamics are not always positive and the team pull in different directions.

Bennett and Dunne (1992) state there are three issues to be taken into account when planning co-operative group work: the interaction between social and cognitive intentions of the grouping; the type of task required; and the match or appropriateness of the task to the children in the group.

Further reading

Bennett, N. and Dunne, E. (1992) *Managing Classroom Groups*, Hemel Hempstead: Simon and Schuster.

Bennett, N., Desforges, C., Cockburn, A. and Wilkinson, B. (1984) *The Quality of Pupil Learning Experiences*, Hillsdale, N.J.: Erlbaum.

Galton, M., Simon, B. and Croll, P. (1980) *Inside the Primary Classroom*, London: Routledge and Kegan Paul.

McNamara, D. (1996) 'To group or not to group' in Pollard A. (Ed.) *Reading for Reflective Teaching in the Primary School*, London: Cassell.

TTA Standard

3.3.3.

Harassment

See *Bullying*.

Homework

There are varying practices in schools about issuing homework. At its most positive it should be seen as an opportunity to establish the practice of study in the home environment, hopefully with the support of others at home. It should be a vehicle for building independent learning. The content should be engaging and possibly relevant to the environment the children are working in. It should not rely on the provision of resources from home (an *Equal opportunities* issue). The amount should be reasonable within a set time limit and the homework should have a clear schedule so that parents know what is expected and can therefore support your expectations. Completed work should be expected and encouragement and praise be given both at home and school. The work should also be seen or followed up in school to show that it is valued and makes a useful contribution to learning. It should be strongly linked to the learning taking place in school and the children should have a clear understanding of what they are expected to do.

Links

Completed work
Equal opportunities
Independent learning

Strategies

- Be clear about the time to be spent on the homework.
- If possible, inform parents of the homework schedule.
- Make sure the work is appropriate for the environment in which they will be working.
- Link the work to what is being learnt in class.
- Expect the work to be completed, mark it or follow it up in class.
- Praise completion and good work.
- Try not to give finishing off as homework.
- If possible, choose something which the children find engaging to do.

Development

Parents and schools have different viewpoints about homework. Some schools believe that their pupils need a large amount of independent study work. On the other hand, some parents believe that academic work should be completed in school and home is for other leisure-type activities. From the pupils' viewpoint, life should be a balance between freedom of choice and study. There is also the question of how old should children be when they are first given homework?

Some schools discourage teachers from sending home 'finishing off' as they believe that either the teacher has not made a good judgement about the amount of work set or that allowing 'finishing off' encourages children to delay work until they get home.

Further discussion could be had on the type of work set. Do we need children to work through twenty examples or should they return prepared to discuss how they worked out one example? Is it possible to complete this particular work in that particular home environment? Some places have set up 'homework clubs' which children attend after school. This is particularly for children whose parents are out at work or who do not have an easy home study environment.

Hayes (1999) offers useful discussion on aspects of homework, including what teachers need to consider when managing homework. He warns that it is time consuming and no substitute for actually teaching children. This leads back to what kinds of things we are asking children to do for homework and why. Muijs and Reynolds (2001) also have a useful and practical discussion on the effective use of homework.

Further reading

The DfES (England and Wales) have issued useful guidance on homework. It can be found on www.dfes.gov.uk (Primary Schools – the purpose of homework).

Hayes, D. (1999) *Planning Teaching and Class Management in Primary Schools*, London: David Fulton.

Muijs, D. and Reynolds, D. (2001) *Effective Teaching: Evidence and Practice*, London: Paul Chapman Publishing.

TTA Standard

3.3.12.

ICT (Information and Communication Technology)

ICT is playing an increasing role within teaching, as society becomes more computer literate and dependent on technology in work and leisure activities. In school there are two strands of technology use. The first is using ICT to support the organization of and quality outputs in managing your teaching. The second is using ICT with pupils to support a range of subject learning and to develop their ICT skills.

Your teaching can be supported by using ICT to:

- plan medium-term (and short-term) documents;
- create and record assessments;
- prepare teaching materials;
- prepare display materials;
- access current initiatives and information (internet).

Working with pupils, ICT can be used to:

- enhance subject learning through use of hardware, software and the internet;
- develop pupils' ICT skills through hands-on experience.

When working with pupils you may be using one computer in the classroom or a suite of computers in a special room. You need to consider carefully the organization of each of these situations to get the most from them.

ICT encompasses a range of hardware including video, computer, overhead projector, tape recorder, programme controlled toys (e.g. Roamer), electronic white boards, all of which can be utilized effectively within the classroom in appropriately planned contexts.

Links

Lesson plan structure
Medium-term planning
Resources

Strategies

- Plan ICT use into your lessons at the medium-term planning stage.
- When working in a suite, structure your lesson, have a clear objective and a teaching input.

- When using one computer in the classroom select relevant programs and carefully organize how children will get a turn. Use children to support skill learning and understanding of program instructions, so you can be free to teach other children.
- Use one computer as a whole class teaching aid.
- Try to provide a range of ICT experiences.
- Use ICT lessons to promote skills.
- Use ICT within lessons to promote subject learning.
- Check it all works before the children arrive.
- Have explored for yourself the programs you are going to use with the children.

Development

With the increase of computer accessibility, particularly to the world wide web and its vast stores of information, we will be forced to reassess our teaching approach to knowledge and the balance between knowledge and skills. Another issue is raised when we ask who has access to computers at home? Will the lack of computer access disadvantage some pupils? Will schools provide after-school access in the same way that they are beginning to provide homework clubs?

A further interesting aspect of computer use by pupils is the programs which they use. What do they learn from them? Does computer use encourage independent study? Do certain programs promote thinking skills? It is important to consider the purpose of a program when you plan to use it in class, in exactly the same way you decide about other activities you ask children to do. There are many types of program including, games, information giving, practice and problem solving.

Student teachers must know how to teach ICT and 'know how to use ICT effectively, both to teach their subject and to support their wider professional role' (DfES, 2002, pp. 7–8). Alongside these expectations for initial teacher training in England, there are other government-funded programmes for practising teachers, for example, the New Opportunities Fund (NOF) and the British Educational Communications Technology Agency (BECTa). Research into children using laptops in the classroom has produced interesting results. Looking into the future, it is possible to envisage every child having access to their own laptop both in school and at home.

Further reading

Ager, R. (2000) *The Art of Information and Communications Technology for Teachers*, London: David Fulton.

BBC Education www.bbc.co.uk/schools (useful for internet resources for children).

BECTa can be found at www.becta.org.uk

Department for Education and Skills/Teacher Training Agency (DfES/TTA) (2002) *Qualifying to Teach: Professional standards for Qualified Teacher Status and Requirements for Initial Teacher Training*, TPU 0803/02-02) London: TTA (weblink www.canteach.gov.uk).

National Grid for Learning (NGfL) www.ngfl.gov.uk (a gateway to educational resources on the internet).

NOF information can be found at www.canteach.gov.uk

QCA site www.qca.org.uk (a useful site for schemes of work).

Teachernet www.teachernet.gov.uk (a teacher resource and staff professional development site, including research).

www.curriculumonline.gov.uk gives easy access to digital learning materials.

TTA Standard

3.3.10.

Inclusion

The first thoughts about inclusion often go straight to pupils with Special Educational Needs, but it is wider than this. It is about all pupils who are at risk of exclusion through:

non-attendance – truancy, long-term illness, long holidays in term time;

disaffection – pupils who attend but take no interest in learning, pupils who bully and their victims;

formal exclusion – pupils whose conduct has been unacceptable in school through persistent defiance of legitimate school rules;

disadvantage – poverty, poor housing, nutrition, poor parenting, children 'looked after' by the state;

pupil mobility – travellers' children, asylum seekers, immigrants.

A social justice view of education takes the view that high quality education for all is an inclusive goal. Social justice has at its roots the idea that economic, racial and gender discrimination are not acceptable. It follows that action needs to be taken to ensure that everyone is able to be included. This implies that strong partnerships and working relationships are needed between parents, pupils, teachers and the different agencies. In the UK, the aim is that mainstream schools should meet the needs of as many pupils as possible.

A useful concept when thinking about inclusion is that of *barriers to learning*. Prejudice and stereotyping are often significant in creating and maintaining these barriers. Pupils who are difficult to teach can evoke negative responses. Rather than thinking about what pupils can achieve we sometimes think of what they cannot do. The ways in which pupils are referred to often gives clues about the mindset of the speaker. For example, 'This is John, he has difficulty in seeing the print in most books so he uses large print books', has a more positive and therefore more inclusive feel, than saying, 'a partially sighted pupil' or 'a blind pupil'. What inclusion is about, is looking for ways of reducing the barriers to learning that exist for pupils who present more of a challenge to school staff.

Links

Differentiation
Equal opportunities
Expectations about pupils' learning
Special Educational Needs
Teaching in teams
Working with other adults

Strategies

Consider the ways you can reduce barriers to learning by:

- Looking for positive attributes in children who are difficult to teach.
- Praising any improvement – rewarding effort and celebrating achievement – e.g. be aware that sitting still for two minutes is a real achievement for some children!
- Being careful about the assumptions you make, e.g. hearing a noise behind you and blaming the 'normal culprit' when he or she is innocent can make it worthwhile for that child to misbehave in future. 'Mr X ain't fair, he's always picking on me' (sic) gives some children the excuse they need not to conform to the rules.
- Using classroom assistants effectively.

- Building your knowledge about the difficulties that cause some children to find learning in school difficult.

Development

Can social inclusion happen? Three ideas – social inclusion, educational inclusion and inclusive schools – are central to UK government policy. These rules are nearly all about improving education provision. Publicly funded schools in England have been set targets for examination success. Alongside this, a rigorous inspection system has required teachers to become better at their work, i.e. to teach *every* pupil more effectively. This has been accompanied by many other measures to begin to enable much greater inter-agency co-operation. Educational inclusion, with the underlying ideas from social inclusion, is about meeting the different needs of as many pupils as possible in mainstream schooling. This happens in many ways. For example:

> Many more classroom and learning assistants are employed to work alongside teachers to support pupils. They work with either individuals because of special need, or to support groups of children with learning difficulties, in particular EAL, but also where standards in English, mathematics or science are thought to be unacceptably low.
>
> Schools have been asked to consider carefully all the ways they can keep pupils in school. Many schools have sought ways to encourage children to arrive on time and to be ready to learn, through things like breakfast clubs. Rewards for a full week of attendance help to reduce unauthorized absence from school. Pupils with unacceptable behaviour, who are in danger of exclusion, may get extra support to keep them where they can continue school learning.

The idea of an inclusive school that will meet the needs of many pupils in a variety of ways; within special classes; through support for individuals; differentiation in the curriculum; and carefully thought through teaching, is an idea that is exciting.

Further reading

Clough, P. and Corbett, J. (2000) *Theories of Inclusive Education: A Students' Guide*, London: Paul Chapman.

Department for Education and Employment (DfEE) (1997) *Excellence for all Children, Meeting Special Educational Needs*, London: DfEE.

Department for Education and Skills (DfES) (2001) *Schools Achieving Success*, London: HMSO.

Lorenz, S. (2002) *First Steps in Inclusion*, London: David Fulton. This handbook has some excellent starting places for making the ideas of social justice work.

See DfES webpages for the most up-to-date information about SEN http//:inclusion.ngfl.gov.uk

TTA Standard

3.1.2.

Independent learning

One of the hardest but most creditable achievements of a teacher is to help his or her pupils along the road to independent learning. Lots of things have to come together to achieve this goal. Pupils need to want to do good work and behave well, because they feel proud to conduct themselves in this way.

They have to learn to be decision makers. They have to become involved in the work they do because they want to do it, not because the teacher says all the time that they have to do it. They have to know what they want to achieve and therefore why they are doing the work. They should want to conduct themselves well around the classroom and to treat each other with respect, because it feels right to them.

As a teacher you need to give them opportunities to exercise these choices, but it will not happen if you just remove all the structures and discipline. Self-discipline comes through recognizing what discipline is. The teacher creates order and gradually encourages more independent decision making through discussion and guidance. There may be 'whole class' stages of this progression or, existing side-by-side, individuals who are ready to take on more responsibility. You, as the teacher, must decide who is ready for 'the greater freedom'.

Links

Active learning

Discipline

Expectations about pupils' learning
Motivation
Problem solving
Self-assessment by pupils
Skill and strategies

Strategies

- Find ways of allowing responsible pupils to be more involved in decisions about their work.
- Discuss expected behaviour and work outputs with the whole class.
- Be clear about why pupils are doing particular pieces of work (purpose as well as objective).
- Ensure certain resources are accessible without permission and, if appropriate, that there are choices about what to use.
- Try to make sure all decision making does not have to pass through you.
- In suitable situations allow pupils to help each other.

Development

Encouraging children to be independent learners is a long-term goal. It is not easy to achieve and you as a teacher will need to think carefully about the 'campaign'. Some children enjoy working at projects and are happy to do so on their own. They always seem to be motivated and engage in anything you offer. Initially, many other children will sit there waiting for you to tell them what to do next. Most children are very teacher dependent. Some teachers like their pupils to be like this, as it offers strong control and they are happy for this to be the status quo for all the year. Whilst control is vital, over and above that, self-control by pupils is even better. If you leave the room will the children continue to work? To achieve this, the pupils need to be able to operate independently of the teacher. This is achieved by promoting a range of skills and understanding. Children need to be confident about their own decision making, they need to be skilled at selecting and using information, they need to know the purpose of the task, they need to want to engage in the task, and they need to have work to move on to if they complete the task early. These are just a few of the opportunities that have to be regularly promoted and praised throughout the year if you want children to manage their own work.

TTA Standard

3.3.3.

Instruction

Letting children know that you're ready to start has to be one of the first things you'll learn to do. You'll need a procedure for gaining everyone's undivided attention. Your instructions need to be brief, clear and positive. Your tone needs to be confident and pleasant. Often you'll need to reinforce your instruction by rephrasing and directing your comments to particular children. For example, first the instruction,

> (*Teacher claps twice.*) 'Can I have everyone's attention, thanks. Martin, Abdul, Shahida, and Susan, look this way, thanks. Now, when I tell you, I want one person from each group to collect the apparatus from me. Everyone else in the group needs to clear away anything that's on your table that's not needed for the experiment. Is that clear?' (*Teacher waits for nods and other indications that the instruction is clear, by scanning each table in turn.*) 'One set of apparatus and one prepared table. Off you go'.

Give generalized instructions once, for example, 'Everyone start work now'. Follow this up by telling a particular child what you want, 'John, start work now'. Don't nag by giving the same instruction to everyone over and over again. Acknowledge those who have heeded your instructions with a smile, a gesture and some quiet praise. Don't fall into the trap of giving the same instruction over and over again as the children soon realize that you are prepared to do this and don't listen the first time.

You'll also be preparing worksheets and other written material which instructs pupils to do something. You'll need to know how best to do this for the whole range of ability. Keeping the language simple, sentences short and being really clear is the key. You may have to prepare two or three versions before you get this right, trialling them with pupils who you know find reading instructions hard. Even then you may have to have the instructions read to some. Another pupil may do this or you might use a taped version or a classroom assistant.

Links

Communicating clearly
Communicating about learning
Demonstration by the teacher
Discipline
Expectations about pupils' learning
Explaining
Independent learning
Purposeful working atmosphere
Relationships with pupils
Timing within lessons
Transitions
Whole class teaching
Working with other adults

Strategies

When instructing children:

- Have a clear signal that gets everyone's attention.
- Be pleasant and confident, stand still, get eye contact, smile, use a clear tone of voice.
- Be precise, be clear yourself what you want done and how it is to be done.
- Be brief.
- Be positive, for example use 'thanks' rather than 'please'. ('Thanks' often demonstrates that you are confident that your instruction will be followed; 'please' can have a pleading quality.)
- Reinforce the instruction through repeating it.
- Deal with anyone who has not yet complied separately.
- Quiet praise to individuals who do as they are asked promptly helps to build a positive working atmosphere.
- Written instructions for your teaching need to be kept simple:
    by the use of direct language, avoid negatives, explain technical terms (use words children know because you've taught them first);
    use short sentences, avoid 'it' or 'they', repeat the subject instead (e.g. 'The cats woke up. They went out'. Beginning readers will find 'The cats woke up. The cats went out' easier to read).
    use a clear type face (Arial is a good example, and at least 12 point);
    use a straightforward layout.

- Check that your written instructions have been understood by pupils.
- Be prepared to trial written instructions to get them to a level that most pupils can read.
- Pupils who find reading hard should have appropriate additional help.

Development

Some instructions are to do with class management. They make the day-to-day organization of the minutiae of teaching and learning possible. Instructions are also part of lesson planning. Both are part of making learning easier. However, you'll also want to consider how you encourage children to make decisions about how, when and where to do things as independent learners.

Further reading

Moyles, J. (1995) (Ed.) *Beginning Teaching: Beginning Learning in Primary Education*, Buckingham: Open University.

Intellectual development

How we learn is a focus of development studies. Development theorists have different, but often complementary, ideas about intellectual growth. Behaviourists, however, offer another idea. There are four theories which you should know about.

The *behaviourist theories* (from the 1920s onwards, with psychologists Pavlov, Skinner and Bandura as the more important names) emphasized change in behaviour as the outcome of learning. The stimulus – response model is clearly seen in much direct instruction, including the management of behaviour.

Jean Piaget's theory of *cognitive development* has two essential elements. He suggests that our minds actively seek to make sense of the world. Our cognitive structures (our minds) are *adaptations* which take knowledge and make it fit with the world about us. He studied many pre-school children. His observations about the mistakes that they make, their misunderstandings which arose from their point of view about how things work, lead him to suggest that 'cognitive development is a process of revision: children revise their knowledge to provide an increasingly better fit to reality' (Keenan,

2002: p. 37) His second big idea was to suggest that we move through four different stages. The knowledge structures used by learners are relatively similar and stable throughout each stage. At the *sensorimotor stage*, birth to about 2 years, 'the infant thinks about the world through their actions on it' (Keenan, 2002 p. 37). The random actions of the child become increasingly more organized and systematic. The child becomes more able to handle abstract ideas and moves into the *preoperational stage*, 2–7 years. At this stage the child becomes able to handle thinking through symbolic representation. In the *concrete operational stage*, 7–12 years, logical thought becomes well established. The *formal operational stage*, adolescence, sees the development of abstract thought. These days this influential theory is increasingly criticized. You'll discover that the child as a solitary learner has little or no support these days.

Lev Vygotsky's *sociocultural* theory of development also sees children as active explorers of the world in which they find themselves. He suggested that it is the social interactions with the people that children meet that make it possible for learning to happen. He also believed that there is a pattern to development, that children move from working with others, to working things out for themselves, characterized by self-talk where the child will talk him/herself through a task. He also observed that parents and teachers, when working with children, tailored what they said, the way they said it and what they did to support the child's development. You will find this currently referred to as 'scaffolding'.

Information processing models and theories seem, after an uncertain start, to be really useful. They arise from computer modelling. *Connectionist* models, that match brain-function to learning tasks, seem promising. For example, the use of advanced organizers to help make connections between what the child already knows and what has to be learned, is one aspect of this theory in classroom use.

All these theories and models have something to offer teachers. It would be impossible to think about teaching and learning without them. Many teachers confirm that children do move through stages. We think of our pupils as active learners. We know that the interventions we make can help or hinder learning and we are beginning to understand how knowledge of the physiology of the brain can help. Clearly this is the briefest of brief outlines; you'll want to learn more.

Links

Active learning
Differentiation
Discipline
Independent learning
Intervention
Linguistic development
Research and its uses
Social development
Thinking skills

Further reading

Keenan, T. (2002) *An Introduction to Child Development*, London: Sage.
Meece, J. L. (1997) *Child and Adolescent Development for Educators*, New York: McGraw Hill.
Muijs, D. and Reynolds, D. (2001) *Effective Teaching: Evidence and Practice*, London: Paul Chapman.
Smith, A. (2001) 'The strategies that accelerate learning in the classroom', in Banks, F. and Shelton Mayes, A. (Eds) *Early Professional Development for Teachers*, London: Open University/David Fulton, explores other ways that theory links to practice.
Sousa, D. A. (2001) *How the Brain Learns*, 2nd edn, Thousand Oaks: Corwin, is recommended for a straightforward introduction to the brain.

TTA Standard

2.4.

Intervention

Intervention is when the teacher engages with groups or individuals in an attempt to move them on with the work they are doing. The most successful interventions enable children to extend their thinking. These usually come in the form of questioning, prompts and requests for explanations from the pupils. Try not to give immediate solutions which is deflating and demotivating. The children will not develop their own problem solving skills if everything is too easy or straightforward. We need children to develop their process skills and take ownership of the work they do.

Intervention can also be considered in the context of behaviour. Much poor behaviour can be prevented by an early intervention into a deteriorating situation. As you get to know a class there will be clues as to the way things are going. For example, a change in the type of noise, known offenders getting restless, or children disengaged from the task because it is too hard. If you sense anything like this, act upon it quickly. If possible do not let the situation deteriorate to the point where you get into disciplinary routines.

Links

Discipline
Group work
Independent learning
Linguistic development
Listening and responding to pupils
Play and structured learning
Questioning

Strategies

- Decide or explore with a child how much help they really need.
- Try to promote children thinking for themselves by choosing a prompt or question type of intervention.
- Try to anticipate problems by early intervention.
- Spot check on children most likely to misbehave (make them aware that you are keeping an eye on them).

Development

Vygotsky (1991), a Russian writer and educationalist who lived in the first half of the twentieth century developed a theory known as the 'zone of proximal development' (ZPD). This term describes the influence the teacher has when working with a child. The greater the improvement when working with the teacher as opposed to the child working on his own, the greater the zone of proximal development, which, Vygotsky thought, was an indicator of potential. An example of this would be an able child dramatically extending and expressing their understanding due to the teacher's intervention with questioning and prompts.

'Scaffolding' is the current term used to describe teacher intervention to support learning. It is the provision of structures by the teacher to enable learning to take place. This might be a light touch such as introducing a task, giving verbal prompts as the task unfolds, or more strongly structured intervention such as a demonstration of the procedure to be followed. Over time a teacher might remove the 'scaffolding' as he/she feels that the concept is established. One can see how scaffolding has close links to Vygotsky's zone of proximal development. Mercer and Dawes (2001) researched how teacher and pupil–pupil language supports learning. They draw upon the theories of Vygotsky and scaffolding to illuminate the dialogues which take place in the classroom.

Wood and Middleton (1975) studied pre-school mothers supporting the play of their 4-year-olds. They observed that there were varying degrees of intervention which they moved between depending on whether their child was stuck in their problem solving or not. Full support was a demonstration, a lighter touch was arranging the materials for assembly, then pointing out the relevant instruction, and lightest of all, giving general verbal prompts. It would be interesting to review what types of intervention are practised in the primary school. It is possible that there are strong parallels to the findings of Wood and Middleton.

Further reading

Mercer, N. and Dawes, L. (2001) 'Dialogues for teaching and learning', in Banks, F. and Shelton Mayes, A. (Eds) *Early Professional Development for Teachers*, London: David Fulton/Open University.

Vygotsky, L. (1991) *Thought and Language* (translation edited by Kuzulin, A.), Cambridge MA: MIT Press.

Wood, D. and Middleton, D. (1975) 'A study of assisted problem-solving', *British Journal of Psychology*, 66: 2, 181–91.

Learning objectives

When planning in the medium- and the short-term it is important to identify what you want children to know and be able to do. A learning objective can be about gaining a new piece of knowledge or acquiring a new skill. The objective of the lesson might be to consolidate or assess a piece of learning. Learning objectives for a lesson might start with the words:

to introduce ... to be able to ... to practise ... to apply ...
to revise ... to assess understanding of ...

They are all focused on what the expected outcome for the pupils is, and involve a process of learning rather than stating the completion of a particular task. The tasks used are the vehicles for the learning. For example, 'to introduce multiplying by 3' is a learning objective as opposed to 'constructing block towers in threes' which does not state what mathematical learning will take place. Some lessons have sub-objectives within the group task phase of the lesson. This allows for differentiation to take place.

Once you have a clear and manageable objective, the planning and teaching become easier and more focused. The assessment becomes easier too, as you know what you are looking for in the children's performance. It is probable that the assessment criterion for the lesson is similar to the learning objective, or is a part of it. It could be appropriate to record whether particular children have met your objective. Certainly it is appropriate for you, as teacher, to evaluate whether the class and groups have met objectives so that you can feed this into your planning (see *Evaluating lessons*). In practice this will mean that you draw from both your scheme and records to plan a follow on lesson.

Links

Active learning
Curriculum
Differentiation
Evaluating lessons
Formative assessment
Lesson plan structure
Medium-term planning

Strategies

- Use sub-objectives if necessary to differentiate work.
- Choose an objective that describes the required learning rather than the task.
- Make the objective reasonably achievable within one or two lessons.
- Plan objectives that build on previous learning.
- Have a cycle of introduction, consolidation and application rather than a new objective each lesson.
- Link learning objectives to assessment criteria.

Development

Children are more likely to learn if your objective is clear and manageable and the purpose is clear to them. Both of these need to be made explicit at the start of the lesson. Some would advocate writing the objective on the board. It depends on whether you think this is an effective strategy for the pupils you teach. Some teachers share their objectives with the parents of their pupils.

A series of carefully constructed objectives should lead to progression in learning and will provide strong evidence for inspection in medium- and short-term planning. You will have to make decisions about worthwhile diversions from your original planning. Maybe the children failed to grasp your objective and you want to revisit it the next day. Maybe a really interesting aspect developed and you feel that the children will learn much by pursuing it. Maybe an event occurred or a child brought a fascinating object into school. These spontaneous situations are no less valid than your planned programme. Evaluate what the children will gain from a change of programme. It is usually a positive learning experience. Just not the one you planned.

TTA Standards
3.1.1, 3.1.2, 3.2.1, 3.3.3.

Learning styles

You'll know that your preferred way of learning is unique. No-one else learns in quite the same way as you do. The same as each child you teach will have a preferred way of learning. Our challenge is to match our teaching to the variety of learning styles[1] that our children may have. And, as far as we can, to give them access to all the learning styles and strategies that they may need to use.

Our five senses give us information about the world, but they don't all contribute equally to the way we learn. We may have a preference to learn visually (perhaps you doodle) – *visual learners*. Or through listening – *auditory learners*. Or prefer touch or whole body movement – *kinaesthetic learners*. Whichever, sensory preferences are important in an individual's learning. Using *VAK* (visual, auditory, kinaesthetic) delivery in balance in our teaching may not be research based, but it does seem to be a really helpful thing to do.

---

[1] Authors use slightly different terms for what is essentially the same idea, for example, learning strategies, cognitive style or strategy, or style constructs. It may be helpful to think about style as what we are born with and strategy as learned.

VAK teaching uses:

- development of visual learning, text plus illustration, graphs, maps, visualization to improve memory, access to CD-ROMs, posters, keywords, videos, demonstrations, memory mapping (e.g. flow charts, story boards);
- development of auditory learning, opportunities to talk about the work, lectures i.e. something to listen to (radio or audio tape) to get the picture, spelling that recalls the pattern through sounds;
- enablement of learning through movement, the opportunity to be active, role-plays, field trips, hand movements and gestures when talking, demonstrations, designs and the making tasks.

Links

Active learning
Differentiation
Displays
Intellectual development
Problem solving
Resources
Thinking skills

Strategies

- Recognizing different learning styles means acknowledging that children will behave differently in lessons, e.g. kinaesthetic learners may seem to fidget more, need to be active in order to learn. This knowledge can help to explain apparent misbehaviour.
- Observe how children react to the different learning styles that you use so that you can extend their ability to learn from each.
- Note that your own learning style preference is likely to be the way you teach. Take account of this when planning by deliberately using other styles in your teaching.
- Help children to recognize that they need to develop different learning strategies through exploring and talking about these with them.

Development

This idea of cognitive styles linked to preferred ways of learning feels right, but the research base is not strong. Riding and Rayner (1998: 9), after an extensive review of the literature, suggests two learning styles – wholistic – analytic dimension; and verbal – imagery dimension, as valid.

Wholistic – analytic individuals tend to organize information in wholes or parts. *Verbal* – imagery style individuals who tend to represent information through thinking verbally or in mental pictures. Gardner (1983) in his analysis recognizes seven kinds of intelligence, known as *multiple intelligences*. It is an attractive theory which suggests that human beings are problem solvers bringing different ways of thinking to different tasks. It is useful to recognize the strengths that you and those you teach have and then to think of ways of helping all of the learners to develop a wide repertoire.

Further reading

Gardner, H. (2001) 'The theory of Multiple Intelligences' in Banks, F. and Shelton Mayes, A. (Eds) *Early Professional Development for Teachers*, London: Open University/David Fulton, pp. 133–41. This chapter draws on Gardner's work from 1983 and work with J. Walters (1985). It appeals to those who like 'common sense' theory!

Riding, R. (2002) *School Learning and Cognitive Style*, London: David Fulton. An authoritative and practical book that covers this area well.

Riding, R. and Rayner, S. (1998) *Cognitive Styles and Learning Strategies – Understanding Style Differences in Learning and Behaviour*, London: David Fulton. The authors provide an excellent introduction to many aspects of learning style, well backed by research.

Smith, A. (2001) 'The strategies that accelerate learning in the classroom' in Banks, F. and Shelton Mayes, A. (Eds) *Early Professional Development for Teachers*, London: Open University/David Fulton, pp. 159–77. This is an excellent summary about many aspects of learning, including learning styles.

Lesson plan structure

The lesson plan is the document on which the detailed organization of your lesson is placed. You will transfer some of your headings from the medium-term planning and you will be making decisions about timing, exact content and resources. Whatever format you use, your lesson plan headings support your thinking on:

- what you want the children to achieve during the lesson (learning objective);
- what you are going to observe and assess (assessment criteria);
- how long you are going to spend on each part of the lesson (timing);

- how and when you are going to group the children (grouping);
- what organization you are going to use (organization);
- what resources you are going to need (resources);
- the specific nature of the content (content);
- prompts for the teaching points you are going to make (teaching points).

It is also a good strategy to have an extension activity for the speedy workers in your class. The plenary or conclusion is where you draw your lesson together and re-establish the objectives so that children know what they have to learn.

It is useful to have the lesson plan within reach during the lesson as a prompt. Putting the lesson plan in a transparent plastic folder will help in keeping it clean and easy to read.

In England the literacy and mathematics lessons have a specified structure, as suggested in the *National Literacy Strategy* (DfES, 1998) and the *National Numeracy Strategy* (DfES, 1999).

Links

Communicating clearly
Communication about learning
Curriculum
Evaluating lessons
Explaining
Group work
Instruction
Learning objectives
Long-term planning
Medium-term planning
Pace
Transitions
Whole class teaching

Strategies

- Always prepare lesson plans so that you are clear and purposeful in your teaching.
- Keep to your proposed timing unless you have an educationally valid reason for adjusting it.
- Make the objective clear to the pupils at the start of the lesson and then return to the expected learning objective at the end.

- Keep your notes brief and easy to read, possibly using bullet points and a highlighter.
- Maintain an assessment focus throughout the lesson.

Development

Muijs and Reynolds (2001) describe two types of lesson: direct instruction and interactive. A piece of learning might go through stages over a series of lessons and this is reflected in the balance of teacher input to pupils involved in task activities. This will be reflected in the timing and content of the lesson. Many people follow a three-part model which starts with whole class teaching, moves on to group work, and then returns at the end to whole class teaching. The first part of this often involves a review of previously taught connected work. The *Numeracy and Literacy Strategies* both have this mix of whole class teaching and group work.

The structure of most lessons will require you to consider and plan for the following:

- learning objective;
- assessment criteria and mode;
- content;
- organization (grouping, timing and resources);
- extension activities;
- conclusion/plenary;
- evaluation.

In addition to planning what the children will be doing, it is important to decide where you will be in the lesson and what you will be doing. This is particularly relevant during the group work where it is possible to spend the whole time 'policing' the classroom when you could be offering teaching input for part of the time. However detailed your planning there will always be differences in the speed at which pupils work, therefore it is important to plan how you will deal productively with the early finishers and those who do not complete their work.

Interesting variations on planning can be found in early years' work. Two good examples of different approaches can be found within the High/Scope and Reggio Emilia projects.

Further reading

Department for Education and Science (DfES) (1998) *National Literacy Strategy*, London: DfES.

Department for Education and Science (DfES) (1999) *National Numeracy Strategy*, London: DfES.

Muijs, D. and Reynolds, D. (2001) *Effective Teaching: Evidence and Practice*, London: Paul Chapman Publishing.

www.ericeece.org/reggio.html Further information about early years in Reggio Emilia.

www.highscope.org An example of a pre-school education programme with worldwide impact.

TTA Standards

3.1.2, 3.3.3, 3.3.7.

Level descriptions

Level descriptions can be found in the assessment section of the English National Curriculum (DfEE, 2000).

They are descriptions of pupils' attainment within each of the attainment targets of the National Curriculum.

> *Each level describes the type and range of performance that pupils working at that level should characteristically demonstrate. The level descriptions provide the basis for making judgements about pupils' performance at the end of Key Stages 1, 2 and 3. At Key Stage 4, national qualifications are the main means of assessing attainment in national curriculum subjects'.* (DfEE, 2000)

In assessing the level of a child's performance, a best fit is made of their achievements against the descriptions provided. These descriptions are drawn from the Programmes of Study (syllabus). It is anticipated that the average 7-year-old in England and Wales should achieve a Level 2 and the average 11-year-old a Level 4.

Level descriptions can be used by schools as part of their internal assessment strategies and reporting requirements, but nationally the children are assessed against these descriptions at the end of Key Stage 1 and 2 in English, mathematics and science. Teacher assessments at these stages must be reported to parents alongside the results of the Key Stage Tests.

Links

Curriculum
Summative assessment

Strategies

- Match a pupil's work to the National Curriculum levels.
- Ensure individual records provide sufficient information to allow a National Curriculum level to be provided in each attainment target.
- Find out what teacher assessment is required during the year and set up assessment and recording systems to evidence this.

Development

Assessing children in this summative fashion on a national scale gives parents, pupils and teachers an indication of their child's performance in relation to all the other children of his or her age in the whole country. From the school's point of view, the performance of pupils in their school provides feedback on how well the school is performing.

It is important for teachers to realize that tests sample a child's knowledge. 'Best fit' assessment indicates that the child is secure in a majority of the criteria but not necessarily all. Teachers' records kept against achievement (criterion referenced procedures) will probably provide the most accurate picture of what a child does and does not know. Even then it is impossible for a teacher to establish exactly what a child knows at any one time.

Further reading

Department for Education and Employment (DfEE) (2000) *The National Curriculum: Handbook for Primary Teachers in England (Key Stages 1 and 2)*, London: DfEE/QCA www.nc.uk.net.
QCA website for tests at www.qca.org.uk/ca/tests

Linguistic development

The response of babies to the pitch, rhythm and cadence of their mothers' voice, not the words, is observed from birth. Between 10–12 months the brain has become familiar with and is able to discriminate the separate sounds (phonemes) of the first language (the one the child hears at home). At about the same time babies begin to attach meaning to words. Speech, producing at first single words, may also start at this time. Learning grammar takes a little longer. Unfortunately, English grammar has many non standard forms. Many 2 and 3-year-olds are about 90 per cent correct, but many may still be learning, through the parents' correction that, for example, 'I hitted (sic) it' needs to be 'I hit it'. The implication is that a language-rich pre-school life will advantage children.

The normal development pattern shows the following milestones:

At birth babies cry to indicate distress, very soon these cries change, the caregiver is able to tell 'contented' or 'playful' cries from other cries.

Between 1–6 months babies hear at first consonant sounds and slightly later vowel sounds. *Cooing* becomes *babbling*. They respond to the child directed speech, *motherese*, that parents (both sexes) give.

6–12 months babbling begins to be like speech, it gradually sounds like the infant's native language.

Between 12–18 months single words – 'mama', 'dada' – come. The infant will point – *gesture* – and use a word to get what he/she wants, which are one word sentences.

Somewhere between 18–24 months there is a great deal of naming, lots of new words are learned very quickly, two-word sentences 'uh uh', 'all gone' – words in the correct order but without the function words – appear.

Two- and three-year olds are learning really quickly through making many mistakes (over generalizations are very common), that parents correct. Three-word sentences appear. Infants learn to take part in conversations.

Up to about 5 years, grammar and syntax (the order of words) gradually become more complex. For example, the question form begins to be mastered. Infants will change how they speak in response to different contexts – home and out-of-the-home speech is heard.

Beyond 5 to adolescence, the number of words in a child's vocabulary increases to 30,000, grammatical construction becomes more complex and, generally, the understanding and use of the full range of language use – things like *pronoun, reference, metaphor, sarcasm* – become established.

Learning to read and write, unlike learning to speak, is not a 'natural' process. Most children have to be taught to read and write. The brain has to learn that marks on the page have meaning. The text is close to speech but not entirely the same. One important difference is the relative permanence of print. It can be read and re-read. Learning to read and write in English, with its complex alphabetic structure, means learning about exceptions as well as rules. There are 44 phonemes, but only 26 letters. Listen to the sound of 'o' in these words: one, women, who, Tom, the same letter can represent more than one sound. Then some sounds (phonemes) can be spelt in different ways, try these: by, tie, bye, high – all ways of representing 'i'. Another potential learning trap is in a word like 'cat' which sounds like one phoneme, even though it is made up of three phonemes *c/a/t*. Poor readers have difficulty with these principles. However, with instruction most children have begun to read well by the age of 8. Writing sometimes lags behind this, and there are considerable differences in skill levels between pupils of the same age.

Links

Differentiation
English as an additional language
Gender
Intellectual development
Research and its uses
Social development

Further reading

Keenan, T. (2002) *An Introduction to Child Development*, London: Sage, Chapter 7 'The development of language and communication' is recommended for understanding speech and listening.

Meece, J. L. (1997) *Child and Adolescent Development for Educators*, New York: McGraw Hill, Chapter 5 'Language development and literacy', is very comprehensive.

Muijs, D. and Reynolds, D. (2001) *Effective Teaching: Evidence and Practice*, London: Paul Chapman 'Literacy', Chapter 15, is an excellent summary on approaches to reading.

TTA Standard

2.4.

Listening and responding to pupils

The classroom is a place where two worlds meet, the world of education and the world of home. As teachers we need to create opportunities for children to link both environments and to contribute from their experience.

By listening and conversing with pupils they will feel valued and are more likely to contribute. If you have developed good dialogue with individuals you will have also created a good setting for learning to take place.

There is a difference between making friends with children and establishing a good working relationship. In a good working relationship there is a two way flow of ideas but the authority of the teacher is maintained at all times. The child will respond better to learning if they sense you are interested in their contributions. At the same time you will need to clearly convey the boundaries of acceptable comment and behaviour to a teacher. In this way the child will be aware and respect the rules of the relationship. You too must keep to these rules. See *Relationships with pupils* for further explanation.

Links

Communicating clearly
Communicating about learning
Culture
Ethnicity
Misconceptions and remedies
Questioning
Relationships with pupils

Strategies

- Create opportunities for pupils to contribute from their own experiences.
- Make time to listen to pupils formally and informally.
- Be interested in children as people as well as in their work.
- Initiate dialogue about what they find hard or easy about work and respond to their comments.
- Develop listening skills with pupils.

Development

Pollard (1997) offers an interesting analysis of the way teachers and pupils communicate in the classroom. He points out that in 1980, as part of the Oracle project, infant children spent 12 per cent of their day listening to and interacting with the teacher. At the time of the PACE project in 1994 this had risen to 40 per cent. In classrooms where Literacy and Numeracy Strategies dominate the curriculum there is a good chance that the whole class teaching element has pushed this figure even higher. This means that it is very important that communication is successful in the whole class teaching phase of a lesson. It not only involves the teacher communicating clearly with the pupils, but also means that both teacher and pupil need to listen and respond. It is very common for the teacher to ask a question, a pupil to respond and then the teacher closes it down with an approving or disapproving remark. This is hardly the structure of genuine discussion and yet this question and answer routine is often claimed to be just that.

Pollard (1997) identifies four forms of listening: interactive, reactive, discriminative and appreciative. The interactive is the genuine discussion, the reactive a response to instruction, the discriminative a listening skill to distinguish sounds, and the appreciative is listening for enjoyment, such as hearing stories, music and poetry. What balance of these occur in your classroom?

Further reading

Pollard, A. (1997) *Reflective Teaching in the Primary School,* London: Cassell.

TTA Standards

1.2, 2.2.

Long-term planning

Long-term planning is the allocation of topics throughout the year for each subject. It is carried out in schools to ensure coverage of legal curricula (e.g. National Curriculum, DfEE, 2000). Planning in this way will ensure that children in different classes in the same year group get an equable programme and it should help with progression of the curriculum from year to year.

If long-term planning is not in place then you need to consult with colleagues and co-ordinators to establish what progression is expected. It is useful to outline your intentions for the year so that you can get a sense of pace and begin to allocate groups of lessons. At this point you will probably move on to medium-term planning. It will be likely that you can use the same long-term structure, with minor adjustments, the following year.

In the National Numeracy Strategy (DfES, 1999) and National Literacy Strategy (DfES, 1998) there are recommended structures for long-term planning.

Links

Curriculum
Medium-term planning
Teaching in teams

Strategies

- Discuss long-term requirements with colleagues and co-ordinators.
- Establish what you are required to cover throughout the year.
- Apportion the topics into half-term blocks.
- Use this outline to develop medium-term plans.

Development

Structured content varies enormously from country to country but there is remarkable similarity of goals in most curricula. An example of a very prescribed curriculum is that legally required in England, The National Curriculum, which has programmes of study for 5–16-year-olds, expected outcomes and attainment targets arranged into ten levels of achievement. Additionally, at Key Stages 1, 2 and 3 (5 years to 14 years), there are tests to measure individual and school attainment. There is also strong guidance for teachers in the form of the *National Numeracy Strategy* (DfES, 1999) and the *National Literacy Strategy* (DfES, 1998) which leaves little room for variation in long-term planning.

Coherent long-term planning is dependent on a whole school approach. This ensures a degree of progression for pupils. No more butterfly paintings in every year for the purpose of demonstrating reflective symmetry! With a prescribed curriculum it is necessary to plan to include what is required for the year. Hopefully this is reasonable in quantity, but at the same time has a breadth and balance of subjects. One suspects that there is always going to be more we would like to teach than we have time for. If the curriculum is not prescribed, these decisions are made by the school or individual teachers.

When schools are large enough to have a two form entry, long-term planning may become a team activity, with year group teachers meeting and planning together. Some schools feel that provision should be totally equable across the year and insist that medium-term planning is shared and delivered at the same time (within the same week). This has the advantage of sharing the workload of planning but can be a challenge on resource provision.

Further reading

Department for Education and Employment (DfEE) (2000) *National Curriculum: Handbook for Primary Teachers in England Key Stages 1 and 2*, London: DfEE/QCA (www.nc.uk.net).

Department for Education and Skills (DfES) (1999) *National Numeracy Strategy*, London: DfES.

Department for Education and Skills (DfES) (1998) *National Literacy Strategy*, London: DfES.

TTA Standards

2.1, 3.1.

Marking

Maybe we need to clearly establish why a piece of work is being marked. What purpose is your marking serving? Are the pupils clear about the purpose? As adults, we seek others to 'mark' draft versions of documents and letters that we write. We have also developed our own checking strategies. There are sometimes opportunities to respond to top copy i.e. the final version, as well. If the top copy is marked then there is an expectation to carry forward marking advice to the next appropriate situation. There are differences between the adult world and the school world, so maybe we should be creating stronger links between school and adult writing situations. For teachers the following questions might arise. Do children get an opportunity to draft work? Do they get the final draft marked or the top copy? How many top copies are expected and what is done with them? What status in the work system does the exercise book have? Do you write on 'top copy'?

In school, marking work is a traditional response to providing feedback, often brought about by large classes generating work faster than the teacher can monitor it. It can form a written record of a pupil's progress. It is also a measure of end product. Grading is a way of marking which allows comparison with classmates or against set criteria. Comments can be encouraging and constructive. Teachers often wonder if children act upon written advice and generally strategies are quite weak in ensuring pupils follow up the advice offered.

Consider also how useful the comments you make are going to be. What effect do comments such as, 'See me' and 'Satisfactory' have on pupils? Is 5/10 good, or did you expect everyone to gain 10/10? How does this mark look when parents examine the books on parents' evening? What sense will parents make of your comments? Sometimes the exercise books are the only evidence they see.

On draft work try to make comments which help children know what to do next. Make comments positive, perceptive and praiseworthy on final work. Try to mark with children present on some occasions and enter into a dialogue about the work. Try to have a quick turnaround on your marking as children are keen to have feedback as soon as possible. Allow time to address errors in a constructive way, maybe through discussion with peers or as a class. Encourage pupils to develop drafting and checking strategies.

You may wish to introduce an element of self-marking in some appropriate situations as this encourages children to seek their own feedback. It will be your responsibility to monitor these situations and get children to understand the significance of correct and incorrect answers. Competitive situations are difficult for children to deal with when self-marking.

Links

Active learning
Competition
Feedback
Formative assessment
Homework
Independent learning
Parents

Strategies

- Allow opportunities for pupils to respond to comments made by you (mark the final draft.)
- Make comments encouraging with suggestions which pupils can act upon.

- Try to mark at least one piece of work during the week with the child.
- Respond to problems quickly by talking about them if possible.
- Mark and return work within 24–36 hours.
- Encourage self-editing and self-marking where appropriate.
- Encourage discussion about errors.
- Consider pupils producing work which they then use in class rather than have it marked.

Development

Marking is a practice which has been handed down almost as a tradition in teaching so maybe it is time to review the practice. A starting point for this might be to ask what purpose it serves in specific contexts. As a summative assessment response it has a clear function. As a formative assessment function there are situations where it may be better to provide alternative feedback of a constructive nature. If marking is used for formative purposes it needs to offer the pupil a way forward which they can act upon, such as, correcting a final draft rather than a top copy. Systems of self-assessment may be a strategy you choose to introduce alongside your own marking.

Hayes (1999) offers good practical advice on marking and feedback and also quantifies the time it will take you. Decisions on marking will eventually affect what outputs you select and how much time you allow to address feedback during lessons. You also need to be clear about your own marking strategies as you may be required to justify them to parents. Consider what messages they are getting from their child, the child's homework, their child's work on parents' evenings and from the school's official policies and communications with them.

Further reading

Hayes, D. (1999) *Planning, Teaching and Class Management in Primary Schools*, London: David Fulton.

Medium-term planning

This is the planning that takes place over a number of weeks. It draws upon the long-term planning or a syllabus. It is the stage where many teachers consider how they will teach an objective and what supporting activities they will require the children to carry out. They will also decide what resources they need to prepare or collect. Deciding on lessons which will generate good display material might be appropriate at this stage. Planning to include ICT could also be considered at the medium-term planning stage. It might be appropriate to differentiate at this stage. There is a balance of detail between the medium-term plans and the lesson plans depending on where you do your thinking about detail of delivery. It is possible that you opt to be well prepared in advance and then adjust your medium-term plans in the light of your lesson evaluations/pupils' performance.

There are examples of medium-term planning in the public domain. A good example is the QCA schemes of work, found at (www. teachernet.gov.uk).

Links

Differentiation
Lesson plan structure
Long-term planning
Resources

Strategies

- Draw upon long-term plans, curriculum documents and syllabii to establish the content of a block of work (e.g. half a term?).
- Consider objectives.
- Consider differentiation (and sub-objectives).
- Consider resources which need to be organized.
- Integrate the use of ICT.
- Plan for display work.
- Co-ordinate across subjects where possible (e.g. symmetry in maths, art and PE).

Development

Medium-term planning has similar issues to long-term planning strategies but some additional ones too. It is at this level that judgements are made about effective learning environments, teaching style and a variety of outputs from the children. Some of this is managing with what you have but there is some room to make choices and be inventive, to try out new approaches and instigate new systems of working with children.

Further reading

QCA schemes, examples of medium-term planning, can be found at www. teachernet.gov.uk

TTA Standards

3.1.2, 3.3.3.

Misconceptions and remedies

Children often misunderstand or develop their own rules for deciding how something should be done. This is part of normal development. Learning things correctly saves children from developing misconceptions. Sometimes children's *ad hoc* rules work in specific situations, but are not correct in others. You need to be clear and correct in what you teach and observant of children's responses. On discovering a misconception it needs to be unlearned and a correct procedure/fact learned. This is harder than learning correctly in the first place! It might be necessary to go back many steps to resolve the problems.

In class, if the misconception arises with the majority of the class when you are teaching them, it is best to stop everyone and go over the point again. If you discover a common misconception when marking homework, it is worth taking a few minutes to address the problem with the whole class in the next lesson. There are various strategies that teachers use to get pupils to address corrections. One possibility is to let pupils discuss errors with each other, under your general supervision. As a pupil works during the lesson, it may be necessary to intervene because you can see misconceptions or errors developing. It is useful to question the pupil at this point about his thinking. Often, on reflection, he will see his error and, if not, you still get some indication of how he is working something out which will enable you to give appropriate advice.

Errors and misconceptions are seen by pupils as mistakes which are seen as a sign of failure. In actuality, they are often signposts on the frontiers of understanding, and as such, indicate where new learning needs to take place. Putting misconceptions right should be given a positive spin in the classroom rather than be tucked away as, 'Five minutes to do your corrections before you go on to page twelve'.

Links

Active learning
Communicating clearly
Consolidation
Expectations about pupils' learning
Intellectual development
Lesson plan structure
Listening and responding to pupils

Strategies

- If a large number of pupils have not understood, stop the lesson and reiterate the point clearly.
- Allow time for pupils to discuss and correct errors.
- Plan time for discussion of mistakes and their causes.
- Question pupils about 'how' they have worked something out rather than launch into an early explanation.
- When marking, certain mistakes can indicate misconceptions which you then need to check with the pupil.

Development

Teacher subject knowledge is an important factor in preventing misconceptions. Before teaching a topic try to research the pedagogic knowledge you require. Initially this can be a large part of your planning load but becomes easier as you call upon your previous experience. Sometimes we fall back on what we were taught ourselves and may be unaware that we too have misconceptions. For example, it is not uncommon to say in mathematics, 'When you multiply two numbers, the answer is bigger and when you divide two numbers the answer is smaller'. Consider the following:

$$\tfrac{1}{3} \times \tfrac{1}{3} = \tfrac{1}{9} \text{ (which is smaller)}$$

and then,

$$\tfrac{1}{3} \div \tfrac{1}{3} = \tfrac{3}{3} \text{ or } 1 \text{ (which is larger)}$$

This is a good example where the rule works with whole numbers, but not when pupils start to extend the number system and deal with fractions. When discussing misconceptions try not to leave pupils without a way forward or with a solution to the problem.

Monitoring pupils' learning

See *Formative assessment.*

More able children

See *Able children.*

Motivation

Finding ways of interesting your pupils in the learning you want them to do is an excellent idea. Helping them to behave in acceptable ways so they can learn is also important. The learner's motivation is a key to this.

In school some children want to learn. Others are less keen! Some children expect to do well. Some are sure that they won't be able to do well. Some learners think that they are successful because they are lucky, others think it is because they work hard, others because they are clever. This helps to explain why some children with similar abilities, achieve more than others.

Motivation is also to do with what individuals *expect* and *want* from the activity you've set. The child's reason for choosing, doing (performing), and keeping at (persisting) the tasks you set will vary.

Motivating pupils to learn is clearly a major preoccupation for teachers. You'll recognize that some pupils have *intrinsic motivation* that comes from internal sources such as curiosity, interest, pleasure, an innate need for mastery and growth. These pupils feel some sense of control over themselves. They are often concerned with the task rather than worrying about what others think about them. Others work better for rewards known as *extrinsic motivation,* as it comes from an external source. These pupils want to succeed perhaps to avoid punishment, or for a high mark, or to please others. For most pupils, indeed most people, both systems operate at the same time.

Maslow (1970) suggested that there is a *hierarchy of needs* that has to be satisfied for people to do well. He suggests that lower order needs like having sufficient sleep and being loved have to be met before learning can take place. An example of this in school might be a child not learning because they are hungry, tired or frightened.

Links

Motivation is a key topic in these links:

Active learning
Competition
Differentiation
Discipline
Expectations about pupils' learning
Independent learning
Learning styles
Listening and responding to pupils
Purposeful working atmosphere
Research and its uses
Rewards
Target setting

Strategies

- Your pupils need to feel valued. Aim for your classroom to be low on criticism and high on warmth (empathy). You and the pupils should celebrate achievement and limit blame.
- Emphasize personal judgement about personal capabilities to encourage pupils to think of their *successes as due to high ability* and attribute *lack of success to lack of effort*. Phrases like, 'You've worked hard' rewards effort; 'You're clever at that now' confirms ability.
- Each child you teach needs to believe that he/she can succeed through effort. This means that you have to set tasks that enable success but require effort.

Development

In Behaviourist theory the emphasis is on managing the learning situation with incentives and reinforcements built in. This standpoint suggests that inner thoughts, feelings or psychological needs are not important, indeed they need not be considered for effective learning to occur. This is often the approach you'll use. Your use of rewards will include, for example, house points, or extra time on the computer, while punishments include loss of privilege. Cognitive theorists, on the other hand, see motivation as a crucial element in learning. The strategies listed above start to deal with aspects of motivation. Motivation is to do with the judgements a child makes about his/her ability to succeed at a task; self-evaluation is informed by what happened in the past, the models friends supply (think of peer pressure) and the feedback the child has had from others.

Further reading

Bigge, M. L. and Shermis, S. S. (1998) *Learning Theories for Teachers*, 6th edn, New York: Addison Wesley Longman, an excellent introduction to theoretical issues.

Maslow, A. (1970) *Motivation and Personality*, 2nd edn, New York: Van Nostrand.

Whitebread, D. (Ed.) (2000) *The Psychology of Teaching and Learning in the Primary School*, London, RoutledgeFalmer. Roland Chapman's chapter (6) on attribution theory is really helpful.

TTA Standard

3.3.3.

Out-of-school learning opportunities

Children learn different things beyond the classroom and they really enjoy school visits. The reality is that they are educationally stimulating and memorable experiences. Visits, part of the day, a day, or longer, can increase a child's competence and independence as a learner. They add an extra dimension to learning that is difficult to achieve in school.

To make the most, educationally, of a school visit you will need to prepare the children beforehand so that they can make sense of what they see. Usually visits are linked to the curriculum, therefore this complements the work going on in the classroom.

During the visit you may ask children to look out for particular objects or events. If you have too much paperwork they will spend their time desperately trying to fill in the answers and miss much of what is going on. Think carefully about exactly what you want them to gain from the visit and then plan accordingly. For example, you might want Year 6 children to write about what it is like to live in an Iron Age round house, having visited the reconstruction. If there is a speaker it would be appropriate for the children to make notes during the talk. You may then ask them to make a list of adjectival phrases whilst they observe the surroundings and feel the atmosphere.

On returning to school you should allow time for follow-up work. This work could vary in form from drama to displays, booklets to creative writing or scientific experiment.

When planning the visit account for: all the costs, including transport; adult supervision; the schedule; informing parents or guardians; what you want and do not want children to bring (in writing); necessary permission (from head teacher, governors, parents and the local authority).

The benefits of taking children on visits greatly outweigh the risks. You will be expected to assess the hazards and make sure that children are going to be reasonably safe. You are advised to read the link in this book on *Safety* as this summarizes some of the actions you should take. There will be specific considerations about hazards and risks for particular out-of-school learning.

As far as you can you will want to ensure that all children can have the opportunity to go. This will mean that the visit is suitable and accessible to all. Extra expense is a huge burden for some parents. Some children have special needs, medical conditions, cultural or religious requirements, that need to be accounted for in setting up the activity. Sometimes you will need to make a hard decision to deny a pupil whose behaviour is likely to be unreliable, the chance to accompany the class. Where children are not able to go, you need to ensure that this aspect of the curriculum is provided in other ways.

Links

Curriculum
Discipline
Expectations about pupils' learning
Long-term planning
Medium-term planning
Safety

Strategies

All these factors need to be considered:

- Include visits in long- and medium-term planning.
- Build in appropriate preparation and follow-up work.

- Get permission from necessary authorities, including parents or guardians.
- Book visit, guides, speakers and transport.
- Organize adult supervision and check health and safety factors including completion of risk assessment.
- Inform parents, guardians, pupils, of schedule and food, money and clothing requirements.
- Have a great day.

Further reading

www.baalpe.org   The British Association of Advisers & Lecturers in PE has definitive information in Safe Practice in Physical Education. This is an excellent starting place for making out-of-school activities safe and enjoyable. See their website for details.

TAA Standard

3.1.5.

Pace

The right pace is achieved when you have the pupils' attention, as learning is most likely to take place when you have their attention. Getting the pace of a lesson right is challenging because children learn at different rates. In oral sessions you will be trying to work at a speed which engages your more able children, but also allows the rest of the class to understand, including those who learn more slowly. This can be thought of as communicating at several levels through the language you use, the content of the work and the general class and individual questions you ask.

If your explanations are too long or you ask too many questions which require long answers, you risk lowering the overall pace. As the pace slows some children stop paying attention, possibly they may begin to misbehave. If the pace is too fast, some children fail to comprehend the teaching points, so they are unable to complete follow-up tasks. In either example, learning does not take place.

Poor behaviour can lead to the teacher engaging in one-to-one discipline talks which further slows the pace of the lesson and other pupils' behaviour can begin to deteriorate. Deal quickly with behaviour problems or sort them out at the end of the oral session. Better still, try and anticipate them and have strategies to forestall them. (For example, sit the naughty children near you in carpet sessions.)

When children are doing tasks, pace is important too. It is useful to give them completion times and targets to remind them of this during the task period. For example, 'You should have answered at least three questions by now' and 'You have ten minutes left, so begin to check your work'. Pupils need to learn to stay on task so make this a clear expectation. Differentiation is important because this allows the task to be manageable.

Links

Completed work
Differentiation
Discipline
Motivation
Questioning

Strategies

- Raise the pace if pupils are restless. Lower the pace if you want to give pupils time to think.
- Extend or shorten oral sessions depending on whether the pupils are engaged in the work.
- Use a mixture of questions that elicit long and short answers.
- Differentiate questions and content to include the range of ability of the class in oral sessions and group tasks.
- Decide when it is time to move on (as pupils begin to disengage).
- Convey expectations about completion of work and time available.
- Check through the lesson that you are maintaining your timing (only change this if you can justify it to yourself).
- Avoid lengthy one-to-ones about misbehaviour in whole class situations (anticipate, then deal with quickly or later).

Development

The Hay McBer report (2000, 1.2.9) states, 'Effective teachers achieve the management of the class by having a clear structure for each lesson, making full use of planned time, using a brisk pace and allocating his/her time fairly amongst pupils'. Getting the pace right by being sensitive as to how the children are responding, and being well organized will go a long way to ensuring the children are on task for a high percentage of your lesson.

Kounin (1970) observed teachers communicating with their classes and found four types of action that teachers took which disrupted the flow of their lessons. He described these as dangles, flip flops, overdwelling and fragmentation.

The dangles left the delivery unfinished.

The flip flop was a change of subject mid-sentence.

The overdwelling was spending too long on a topic already grasped by the pupils.

The fragmentation was splitting up the work into so many small steps that the pupils lost the purpose of the lesson.

The general impetus is to increase the pace to ensure pupils' attention and reasonable behaviour. It is worth considering whether the pace matches the task. It would be quite easy for pupils to abdicate from higher order thinking when the teacher moves on too quickly and does not allow enough time to work something out.

Further reading

Hay McBer (2000) *Research into Teacher Effectiveness: A Model of Teacher Effectiveness*, London: DfEE (www.dfes.gov.uk/teaching reforms/leadership/mcber/).

Kounin, J. (1970) *Discipline and Group Management in the Classroom*, New York: Holt Reinhart and Winston.

TTA Standard

3.3.7.

Parents

Parents, the people who care for the pupils in your class, have rights and responsibilities. Your respect for them is central to establishing and maintaining a working relationship. See the entry on *Communication with parents* for further information and reading.

Who are parents?

This depends on the circumstances. The child's natural parent(s) may not always be the person/people with responsibility. Step-parents, relatives, co-habitees of step-parents and relatives and adoptive parents may all take on parental responsibility. In the UK, foster carers and people employed by Local Education Authorities to look after children subject to residence orders or care orders are not treated in the same way by Education Acts, but in practical terms will often be treated by school authorities as taking parental responsibility.

What is parental responsibility?

These are all the rights, duties, powers, responsibilities which a parent of a child has by law. For example, in the UK it is a parental responsibility to ensure that school-aged children attend school.

What is parenting style?

The way that children are dealt with at home will make a difference to their response to teachers and peers. Some parents are very strict and controlling: they adopt an authoritarian style. This may mean that children have too little freedom to develop. Some give children opportunities to make mistakes and support their development in many ways: this authoritative style enables development. Others give in to the child's whim: an indulgent style may mean that the child has no boundaries within which to develop. Some seem not to care to deal with their child's development: an uninvolved style may mean that the child has no boundaries and little home support. You will draw your own conclusions about the influence of parenting style from the way the children you teach learn and behave.

Links

Communication with parents
Relationships with pupils

Physical development

Factors such as cultural practices, nutrition and experiences all influence physical growth and development. Heredity is likely to determine eventual height and physical appearance. This helps to account for the considerable physical differences you'll see between children of the same age.

Human growth is comparatively slow. It is not until between a year and fourteen months that most children can walk unaided. Physical development is at its most rapid in infancy, children get taller and stronger more rapidly between 0–5 years. Growth slows from about age 6 until the onset of puberty. Until puberty differences in height, weight and muscle mass between girls and boys are slight, for example, both sexes can be expected to have a similar ability to run and jump.

The onset of puberty brings changes in the sexual characteristics. It is worth knowing about the changes that occur, as the psychological effects are considerable for some children. Parents and pupils are often surprisingly uninformed about puberty. With the consent of the parents, as a teacher you are often well placed to give accurate information to your children. The variation between the onset of puberty and the rate of growth between individuals is considerable. There will be some children in primary school who start to go through these changes at a very young age e.g. a few girls menstruate from 7 years old. Physical development at this stage is complex. There are changes in the reproductive system, in the cardio-vascular system and the lungs with an affect on the respiration system and the size and strength of many muscles in the body. Often there is a 'growth spurt'.

In secondary school there are students of the same age who are young men and women, working alongside others who are still children. Although this is perfectly normal it can be a source of considerable anxiety both to adolescents and their parents. The growth spurt may start as young as 9 for some boys, but may not happen until 15. While girls may start as young as 7 or 8, but may not until they are 12, 13 or 14. The average, though, for boys is around 12 and between 10–11 for girls.

Links

Emotional development
Intellectual development
Linguistic development
Research and its uses
Social development

Further reading

Meece, J. L. (1997) *Child and Adolescent Development for Educators*, New York: McGraw Hill.

Oates, J. (Ed.) (1994) *The Foundations of Child Development*, Milton Keynes, Oxford: Open University and Blackwell. Ken Richardson in Chapter 6, 'Interactions in development' is an interesting introduction to some of the complexities in this area.

TTA Standard

2.4.

Play and structured learning

The role of play in human development is much debated. It may be a need which continues through life but takes different forms as we grow older. Within the education system play is seen as a need for young children and in most curricula there is an expectation that children will have opportunities to play. Play situations can range from child controlled play, through varying degrees of teacher controlled situations.

Teachers set up various types of play situations. First there is completely free play where children choose what they are going to do and what equipment/toys they are going to use. This is akin to children's experience in the early years at home and in play school. In the primary school this can still be seen in reception classes and, of course, all the way through school, at break-times. In the classroom/nursery, a second common practice is for the teacher to set out equipment which is relevant to a theme/objective which is being promoted and there may even be an indication of who is to use the equipment, but no task is set. An example of this further up the primary school can be seen when teachers prepare interactive displays. Open task situations such as this can be followed up by the teacher joining a group and intervening with questions and related teaching points. The third situation is when the teacher sets a task with the selected equipment.

Finally, the teacher may initiate and control the whole task. (Setting the task without selecting the equipment moves us into the territory of problem solving: 'What shall I use to solve this task?') As you can see, through this range there is a move towards structured learning similar to that found in classes of older children. The expectation to attend and respond to the teachers' agenda is gradually developed. This does not mean that free play situations should be eliminated.

Links

Curriculum
Displays
Early learning goals
Emotional development
Intellectual development
Intervention
Problem solving
Resources
Social development

Strategies

- Decide whether the situation is going to be entirely free, or if equipment and/or task are going to be set.
- How much teacher intervention is planned? Is it at the beginning or towards the end of the task?

Development

One cannot mention young children and play without paying due respect to the philosophies of educational giants such as Montessori, Steiner and Isaacs, whose theoretical standpoints are highly influential in nursery education. Collecting empirical evidence on the exact role of play in learning has proved difficult, partly because the word encompasses many different types of activity and partly because researchers look for different outcomes. A useful account of theory, past research and research with teachers of 5-year-olds can be found in *Teaching Through Play* (Bennett *et al.*, 1997). Play may have links with assimilation of learning and creativity, but in education systems where immediate learning is expected on prescribed objectives, play can come under pressure for not delivering tangible results. Play must be considered within the early years' curriculum and teachers should decide on its value and create a range of opportunities from free play through to structured tasks.

An issue to consider is whether primary classrooms are too structured. Is there a danger that structure stifles spontaneity, decision making and creativity? With more prescribed curricula it is tempting to justify rigorous target setting for each lesson so that children progress through the curriculum at a rapid rate.

Further reading

Bennett, N., Wood, L. and Rogers, S. (1997) *Teaching Through Play*, Buckingham: Open University Press.
DfEE/QCA (2000) *Curriculum Guidance for the Foundation Stage*, London: DfEE/QCA.

Problem solving

Life is full of problems that need to be solved therefore this is a process which needs to be present in education. Much has been written about the skills and processes involved in problem solving in different subjects. Whether you see it as a way into new work or as an opportunity to apply acquired knowledge, it is an essential life skill and a rationale for gaining new skills and knowledge (using what you learn).

Sometimes when teachers provide children with problems and investigations the children fail to get started or do not come up with a solution. As in real life, no-one can immediately solve all problems. Often time is needed to try different strategies or make a useful mental link or acquire new relevant knowledge. What children do need is knowledge of the strategies or processes which can be used to try and solve problems. These need to be taught overtly just like the rest of the curriculum. Getting started, sorting the data, seeking patterns, linking to what you know, trying out a theory, testing a theory, etc. are all ways of working which we have to help children understand and use.

Links

Active learning
Explaining
Group work
Independent learning
Intervention
Listening and responding to pupils
Skills and strategies
Thinking skills

Strategies

- Include problem solving in medium-term planning in suitable subjects.

- Help children with processes by teaching and discussing them (as lesson objectives?).
- Do 'whole class' problem solving to start with to demonstrate the thinking processes they need to use.
- Use problem solving to consolidate work and to assess whether children have a working knowledge of a piece of learning.
- Or, use a problem to introduce a topic and engage interest.
- Develop a range of verbal 'prompts' to help children think about their work when they are stuck (which can be in the form of a set of questions).
- Reassure pupils that work often leads to 'dead ends' and that they sometimes need to go back and pick up a new thread.

Development

You can set problems that have a single step and one solution such as, 'Which two paints do you mix to create orange?'. Other problems have many steps before you arrive at the solution. A common error that children make is to find a solution but not check back to see if it answers the original question. For example, in a question which asks for the number of minibuses needed to transport a class of 39 children to the swimming pool when each bus holds 12 children, a child answers, 'You need 3.25 minibuses. A further step in rounding up needs to be taken to give a realistic answer of 4. A further set of problems are those that are open ended. Sometimes these open-ended problems are known as investigations. They also offer the opportunity for children to make decisions and pose questions. There are opportunities within them to decide which lines of enquiry you will pursue. Children may have different solutions and even more questions in this type of enquiry. All these forms of work require children to develop a process of tackling problems which brings together use of their prior knowledge and generic strategies for what to do next. Fisher (1987) writes about the processes primary school children employ in problem solving. His strategies are in the form of a series of child-friendly questions.

Further reading

Burton, L. (1984) *Thinking Things Through*, Oxford: Blackwell.
Fisher, R. (1987) *Problem Solving in the Primary School*, Oxford: Blackwell.

Purposeful working atmosphere

It is important to have a purposeful working atmosphere because it is in this environment that learning is most likely to take place. There is also the implication that children will be engaged in work they see as meaningful and are therefore motivated to do. Many factors come together to create this kind of environment. A purposeful working atmosphere is often observed in classrooms where the teachers believe that children should be independent learners; it appears that this is more likely to be achieved if the children see the work as their work, rather than something that is totally imposed by the teacher. Others would argue that this is not true; it is purely a matter of clarity of purpose and good organization that create a purposeful working atmosphere.

Whichever view you hold, to move towards achieving a purposeful working atmosphere it is important that all the children understand what they are working towards and that the work is at a level in which they can engage and contribute. This will assist in helping them to stay on task. It is the teachers' responsibility to motivate the children to complete the task and complete it well. The teacher must make it clear what standard of work, behaviour and style of working they expect in their classroom. This is often done quite overtly when the teacher first begins to work with the class and is gently reinforced over a period of time.

Links

Communication about learning
Discipline
Equal opportunities
Expectations about pupils' learning
Expectations of pupils' behaviour
Listening and responding to pupils
Motivation
Relationships with pupils
Target setting

Strategies

- Clear expectations of how the children are going to go about the work.
- Well differentiated work (lesson planning and formative assessment).

- Attainable and clearly stated objectives, shared with the children.
- Generate an enthusiasm in the children to do the work (motivation).
- Well organized resources.
- Encourage children to take responsibility through decision making about their own work.

Development

Underpinning a purposeful working environment will be a well established relationship between the teacher and the pupils. The pupils should understand that the teacher is interested in what they are doing and know the rules of conduct and work procedures in the class. In return, the teacher provides a stimulating environment, fairness of action and a genuine interest in the work and welfare of his/her pupils.

Physically, the classroom should be clean, tidy and warm, with stimulating display material on the walls and shelves. Children will want to be there. They may even have a sense of ownership and contribute by being monitors/helpers.

The teacher will also ensure that the work environment is non-threatening. It will be a place where children feel that they are able to contribute, even if it is only a tentative suggestion. There will be no fear that they are going to be ridiculed by their peers or rejected by the teacher.

TTA Standards

2.7, 3.2.4, 3.3.8.

Questioning

There are several different types of questioning which elicit different forms of response from pupils. The most common form of questioning observed in the classroom is: teacher asks question, pupil gives short response, teacher gives a short response indicating whether he/she approves of the answer, or thinks that it is wrong. This closed questioning is designed to get a simple, often anticipated response, for example 'What is the capital of France?' or 'What is 9×7?'.

Open questions are those where a pupil might offer any one of a range of answers or explanations. For example, 'How could you work that out?' or, 'What do you think happens next in the story?'. Open questions promote children's articulation of their thinking.

Children are very good at working out whether they have given a successful answer. They read the teacher's body language and interpret the teacher's responses. For example, if a teacher frowns slightly or says 'Are you sure?', they will assume they have given a wrong answer and will often offer an alternative response. However, 'Are you sure?' might be the teacher being genuinely interested, asking the pupil to justify their response. Children, however, quickly get used to the pattern of your questioning.

When children are struggling, sometimes it is a better strategy to question what they have done so far or suggest a way forward. These are 'prompt' questions and help children to articulate their thinking. Often this allows a child to see a way forward for themselves. As you work with your pupils you should increasingly expect them to justify their responses.

Links

Active learning
Communication about learning
Demonstration by the teacher
Explaining
Feedback
Independent learning
Instruction
Intervention
Listening and responding to pupils
Pace
Thinking skills
Whole class teaching

Strategies

- Use a range of question types.
- When you want to increase the pace of an oral session use closed questions.
- When you want to explore children's thinking and encourage their explanations, use more open questions.
- To promote consolidation of understanding ask children to talk about what they have done.
- If a child is stuck, use a 'prompt' question.

- Experiment with the balance between your information giving and your questioning.
- Increase the level of demand for explanations and justification as appropriate to individual's progress.

Development

Perrot (1996) offers an analysis of questioning in whole class oral situations and offers strategies for use of different types of questioning, including higher order questions which are aimed at eliciting responses which require pupils to think. Such questions might require them to analyse information, offer informed opinion or make new links between known facts.

Hayes (1999) gives a useful summary of the use of questioning by the teacher and then moves on to the importance of pupils developing their own questioning skills. It is very much the teacher's responsibility to create a classroom environment where it is alright to ask questions. It is very easy to misuse questions about work in order to discipline poor behaviour or inattentiveness (Galton, 1996). This leads to a reluctance to answer academic questions, so make behaviour questions/statements clearly about behaviour only.

Further reading

Brown, G. and Wragg, E. (1993) *Questioning*, London: Routledge.
Galton, M. (1996) 'Ambiguity in learning' in Pollard, A. (Ed.) *Readings for Reflective Teaching in the Primary School*, London: Continuum.
Hayes, D. (1999) *Planning Teaching and Class Management in Primary Schools*, London: David Fulton.
Perrot (1996) 'Using questions in classroom discussions', in Pollard, A. (Ed.) *Readings for Reflective Teaching in the Primary School*, London: Continuum.

TTA Standard

3.3.3.

Recording individual progress

When considering what you are going to record, always be clear about the purpose, as this will help you identify what is most useful to collect evidence about (assessment criteria).

Recording individual progress happens at various levels and for different purposes. In the classroom you will probably wish to keep 'informal notes' about children meeting specific objectives or having difficulty. This is done to enable you to keep track of how each child is progressing. These 'notes' will feed into your lesson planning and could be used to inform a more official record.

At the next level there will be particular information which needs to be passed on to others such as the SENCO (Special Educational Needs Co-ordinator), the next teacher, parents, school records, or the next school. Schools often decide the nature of the information they wish to send or receive.

A third level is official and legal. There are requirements to report on individual progress to parents and Local Education Authorities (LEAs). In England there are also legal requirements for information on annual reports to parents and teacher assessment within the key stage assessment procedures (see *Summative assessment*).

Links

Formative assessment
Marking
Parents
Special Educational Needs
Summative assessment
Target setting

Strategies

- Before teaching decide what assessment system you will run.
- Before teaching devise appropriate recording formats.
- Choose manageable assessment criteria and ones that will inform you about children's understanding.
- Check what information needs to be collected over the long-term (half-term, term, year). Devise a strategy to ensure that you can acquire this evidence.
- Build into your planning a strategy to deal with the findings of your assessments (i.e. when will you deal with individuals who do not understand this work; day-to-day, week-to-week, medium-term?).

Development

For teachers who spend a complete year with the children in their classes, recording is more likely to be done in the medium-term.

These teachers have a wealth of experience against which to measure those students who lie outside the normal range of progress. As a student teacher, recording serves several purposes. One purpose is to track individuals and inform the class teacher about their progress at the end of the practice. Another is to ensure you develop assessment procedures as part of the teaching cycle. Your recording will provide evidence for you and your mentor of how consistent you are in collecting information about individuals and how you use that information. One purpose of teaching practice is that it is the place where you will need to try out a variety of assessment and recording methods, which will then be required for use when you get your own class to teach.

TTA Standard

3.2.7.

Relationships with pupils

The way that you work with your pupils, what you say to them, how you treat them and the respect you show them, helps to build your reputation. If you think back to your own school days, you will recall the teachers you liked and those you disliked. You will be with the children in your class every school day for a whole year. As well as the children expecting you to teach them, they will expect other things from you. Beyond achievement in their own work, they would like you to be approachable, take an interest in them and know about them as people. Particularly for the younger children, you are a cross between a parent and a representation of authority. They will value firmness but will appreciate approachability.

Your personal code of conduct will be based on your understanding of ethical principles, legal requirements, contract of employment, the job and role and the expectations that other colleagues, parents and the community beyond the school have. There are some things that are never acceptable, for example, a sexual liaison with someone you teach, advocating illegal acts, or promoting a particular political party. You should be cautious about any meetings with any pupil on a one to one basis; for example, 'Come in on Saturday morning to help me finish this project'. Always make sure that several children or other adults are around. It would be naïve not to safeguard your professional reputation.

Links
Bullying
Child protection
Emotional development
Equal opportunities
Inclusion
Listening and responding to pupils
Motivation
Purposeful working atmosphere
Social development
Teachers' employment and conditions
Values and ethos

Strategies
Recognize that children have expectations about you. All you have to do is teach well and treat them fairly. If past experience of teachers was poor, your task initially will be much harder. Take account of learners' feelings and emotions. What are their anxieties? How motivated are they?

- Share your excitement and enthusiasm for learning.
- Respect your pupils by preparing to meet their different needs. Accept their standards, either high or low, as a starting place for better things.
- Praise effort, celebrate achievement on an individual basis.
- Set able pupils higher targets and encourage discussion.
- Be aware of your own views about race, gender, class and special needs. Make sure that you treat pupils fairly by sharing out your time fairly.
- Avoid remarks that may be received as negative. Be careful that your jokes are not at someone's expense.
- Be approachable, teaching is a two-way process; promote genuine discussion.
- Be yourself, teaching does use acting skills but pupils very soon know more about you than you often know yourself.

Development

Sometimes the way we are required to deal with pupils conflicts with our personal set of values. For example, you may not care about whether a pupil is in school uniform or not, but in your school it is the rule, so you're expected to enforce the school dress code. This is where you need to uphold professional standards. If there is a mismatch between your views and school policy you must seek to make your case at policy level, not at pupil level.

Further reading

Cowley, S. (1999) *Starting Teaching: How to Succeed and Survive*, London: Continuum.

Thody, A., Gray, B. and Bowden, D. (2000) *The Teacher's Survival Guide*, London: Continuum.

TTA Standard

3.3.1.

Research and its uses

'What research questions should I be asking?' 'What's worth spending precious time on?' Research questions can arise from what you do in your teaching, through questioning your own knowledge about the content of your subject. You will want to find out why some of your teaching is more effective, some less so, and more about the ways in which children learn best. In your school, you might ask, 'What are the best solutions to the challenges here?' Beyond the school you need to know about current issues so that you can question these. Furthermore, it is a proper and a legitimate use of your time. In England research is a Teacher Training Agency (TTA) standard. It is also part of the General Teaching Council's professional code. For your own professionalism it is important for you to be a learner, risk taker and an explorer, after all, this is what we ask children to do. Research for teachers has several aspects: it supports subject knowledge; how we teach (pedagogic knowledge); and also addresses wider educational issues.

Knowledge about the subjects you teach needs to be kept up-to-date. From time to time curriculum development means that you will

need to learn something new. You need to know what children may
find hard to learn so that you can pay extra attention to making this as
easy and interesting as possible for them. To do this you'll research
subjects thoroughly; you'll make sure that what you are teaching is
accurate.

As a teacher you have expectations about the children in your
class. You will be thinking all the time of ways that you can make
the concepts and knowledge they need really interesting and easy for
them to learn. You will want to know that the way you teach is as
effective as possible and your reflections about the relationships
between teaching and learning will lead you into doing research
on the subject, in order to be more knowledgeable about it. You
will want children to look forward to your lessons, even when the
ideas are difficult. At first you may plan some of your teaching
following ideas that work for other teachers. With experience your
repertoire of teaching approaches will expand. The research
question is, 'What works for me?'. You will want to put yourself in
a strong position to argue for your approach. You will be basing
your teaching on something other than a hunch, or 'it works
because it works'. Your research will take the form of assessing the
effectiveness of your actions through the evidence you collect from
learning taking place in your own classroom.

Keeping yourself informed about issues beyond the classroom
means that you will know what policies are likely to impact on
your work. An international perspective is important as well.
Reading the education press and professional journals alerts you
to the world beyond the classroom. This will often inform your
reflection on your own practice. Your information will also be used
in discussions with colleagues.

Links

Active learning
Continuing professional development
Independent learning
Teachers' employment and conditions

Strategies

- Question your own ways of knowing through reading, networking
  and keeping up-to-date on issues.

- Read the research:

  read critically and find alternative views to make the most of research;

  survey the literature by reading the summaries rather than whole articles;

  use databases, both the British Educational Index (BEI) and Educational Resources Information Centre (ERIC) for example, to locate the areas that interest you;

  carry out searches for particular information through search engines like www.google.com; be aware that the WWW (World Wide Web) has both splendidly authoritative sources and the most awful rubbish available on it, with all shades in between.

- Network with others who are interested in similar areas through local professional groups, local university contacts and national and international associations.

- In the UK use the websites of official bodies such as the TTA, Department for Education and Skills (DfES), Office for Standards in Education (Ofsted), Qualifications and Curriculum Agency and British Educational Communications and Technology Agency (BECTa) to identify the issues that they think important. These bodies are policy makers so the research they support and commission is often related to a particular view.

- Use university and teacher centre libraries to obtain access to the best research.

- Seek sponsorship for classroom enquiry and continuing professional development (e.g. DfES, TTA, Education Action Zones all offer opportunities for funding).

Development

As you teach you will be thinking about the research you have read and making connections with your work. You may well start to develop an interest in a particular aspect of teaching. At that point you will want to ask your own research questions. When you are ready to carry out some research of your own, training and support is offered by universities. You may be able to fund this through your school's staff development fund, or through grants made for this purpose from a variety of sources. Teachers who choose to research practice often find it very time consuming but they also admit that the challenge was worthwhile and invigorating.

Further reading

Banks, F. and Shelton Mayes, A. (Eds) (2001) *Early Professional Development for Teachers*, London: Open University/David Fulton. Section 3 has an interesting selection of articles about research.

Matherson, C. and Matherson, D. (Eds) (2000) *Educational Issues in the Learning Age*, London: Continuum.

Pring, R. (2000) *Philosophy of Education Research*, London: Continuum.

Sayer, J. (2000) *The General Teaching Council*, London: Continuum.

www.becta.org.uk

www.canteach.gov.uk the TTA site.

www.curriculumonline.gov.uk

www.DfES.gov.uk lists Best Practice Research Scholarships sponsored by the DfES.

www.ofsted.gov.uk

www.qca.org.uk

www.teachernet.uk.gov outlines current DfES commissioned research.

TTA Standard

1.7.

Resources

Good resources can provide a stimulating start to a lesson as well as offering useful visual images (a picture is worth a thousand words?). Well-resourced practical work enhances the learning environment because children are able to work in a physical as well as a mental medium.

There are two kinds of resources; those that are readily available in your classroom from day to day, and those that you have to acquire or make. This second group need to be considered when you do your medium-term planning to allow you time to assemble them. The second group of resources might include, posters, a collection of objects, a set of demonstration number cards, a collection of artefacts from a historical period or books and videos for a particular topic.

When you are considering the resources you are going to use, take into account social, cultural and gender implications, and ensure that you provide a fair curriculum for your children. Schools are not wealthy and sometimes resources such as books can be quite old. Check that the textbooks you use are appropriate for children growing up in this day and age. It is part of your role as a teacher to ensure that you monitor the resources available to children in your classroom.

Links

Culture
Differentiation
Equal opportunities
Formative assessment
Purposeful working atmosphere
Social development

Strategies

- Plan at medium-term level for resources you need to make or acquire.
- Try and find resources that illustrate well the teaching points.
- Create a visually stimulating environment. (interactive too).
- Use a variety of resources to capture attention.
- Use resources to bring the outside world into the classroom (art, pictures of other countries, posters with messages about the environment etc.).
- Update and check that your resources are appropriate for modern society.

Development

Over a century ago, when education for very young children was new territory, Froebel devised a series of educational toys which, through play, would promote children's understanding of logical and mathematical relationships. This is early evidence of the recognition that resources can aid children's learning. Nowadays, in primary schools there are a wide range of resources on offer to support children's learning. Unfortunately, schools never seem to have quite enough money to buy all the resources they would like. Many teachers are ingenious at making their own resources. These are often the most effective too because the teacher knows what is appropriate for his or her children and what is going to be effective in illustrating what he or she wants to teach. Good ideas for teachers are now abundant on websites as well as in books. When planning to use resources, make sure that they are prepared, so time is not wasted in lessons. When planning to use resources select those which support the learning that you expect to take place. Occasionally resources can be used as an open-ended stimulus. Sometimes children bring things into the classroom which can be opportunities for spontaneous learning.

When developing independent learning there will be times when you expect children to make decisions about what resources they think are going to help them carry out a task. How are your resources organized? Are they accessible to the children? Do they need to ask you for everything or are certain things openly available? How do you organize for resources to be kept tidy? Is tidiness an expectation of every individual or do you have monitors? If you have monitors does this mean children can leave things out because they know others will 'clear up'? Think through the implications of your organization.

Further reading

An example of a teacher's resource site on the web can be found at:
www.ambleside.schoolzone.co.uk/flashindex.htm an award winning school
   site.
www.curriculumonline.gov.uk

TTA Standards

3.3.1, 3.3.8.

Rewards

Do not undervalue the power of positive comment. As human beings we respond to praise and encouragement. The need to be 'overt' with young children sometimes makes this feel excessive but, as long as the pupil's action is worthy of praise, be unstinting with it. Praise does wonders for pupils' confidence and motivation. It is a challenge in any classroom to avoid being negative. When only positive comments are heard aloud it has the effect of creating a positive classroom environment where children are happy to work. If you have to tell someone off, it is appropriate to speak to them quietly on a one-to-one basis and always leave them with a way forward.

Rewards can be verbal or non-verbal, such as a smile, or placing good work on display, or asking them to tell the rest of the class about their work in the plenary.

Rewards can also be more tangible. They can be part of a behaviourist approach to learning. Good behaviour and work is reinforced by rewards (points, sweets, praise, sharing work with a wider audience, etc.). Rewards can be used by the teacher as an overt indicator of quality work. Be sure to reward quality work rather than a large quantity of mediocre work.

Links

Competition
Discipline
Motivation

Strategies

- Try to make sure all whole class comments are either positive or instructional.
- Deal with poor work/behaviour on a one-to-one basis.
- Use rewards in appropriate situations such as:
    good behaviour;
    good effort;
    a small step of improved performance;
    quality work.
- Be fair in offers of rewards.
- Do not withdraw rewards already given.

Development

Some schools use powerful reward systems to instigate new behaviour and work patterns. One such system is called, 'Smarties in the Jar', with the children banking points through the week for good behaviour and work, then the best group and individuals are rewarded with treats, such as extra break time. Cumulative good responses from a class might be rewarded with a school visit. This is a strong, behaviourist strategy to encourage change, which utilizes the desire for reward and the willingness to compete.

Behaviourist research (Skinner, 1974) indicates that removal of rewards does not eliminate poor behaviour. Skinner also believed that rewards need to be frequently reinforced to establish good behaviour.

Further reading

Skinner, B. (1974) *About Behaviourism*, London: Cape.

Safety

Everyone who works in school has a *duty of care* to keep children safe. For teachers the duty of care implies more than acting as a 'good and careful parent'. In the UK, and many other countries, teachers have a statutory obligation to assess risks in all types of situations. Risk assessments involving physical safety are likely to be high on most schools agendas. You will see teachers taking care over how pupils are trained to behave when faced with physical danger, however slight that may be. For example, youngsters will be trained to carry scissors in such a way as to minimize danger. Beyond this, where the welfare of the pupil is central to the values and ethos of the school, action may be taken to address wider issues. These may include sex education, anti-drugs education, anti-smoking education, anti-bullying policies, healthy eating education, environmental education, road safety, personal protection, education for sustainable development, or whatever is currently of general concern.

Risk assessment

A hazard means anything that can cause harm, while risk is the chance that someone might get hurt. Risks can be high or low. Your task is to make sure that the precautions you take mean that the risk is small. Getting rid of some risks is an obvious choice. But making children's life entirely hazard free is not an option. Helping children to make the right choices about risk is part of our job. We need to expose children to hazards so that they can begin to make choices about risk for themselves. At the same time you need to make sure that the risks are as small as possible so as to avoid accidents. The law says that you have to take reasonable precautions.

Usually, the younger the child the higher the risk of harm. But at any age you'll have some children who are not very sensible about risk. You'll need to take especial care with them. Think too about the needs of children with disabilities. Looking carefully at hazards in the subjects you teach and in the space in which you work, should be a regular part of your work. Think about the children and the degree of risk to which they should be exposed. You'll need to be especially careful when you take children away from school on visits. For out-of-school activities you will be required to complete a risk assessment form.

There are five steps in risk assessment.

1. Look for hazards.
2. Decide who might be hurt and how.
3. Evaluate the risk to decide about precautions.
4. Record your findings.
5. Review your assessment at regular intervals or at end points for one-off events.

Links

Child protection
Discipline
Out-of-school learning opportunities
Purposeful working atmosphere

Strategies

- Know what hazards are associated with the subjects you teach.
- Know how to minimize the risks in the subject.
- Agree with the children what the safety rules for movement around the classroom and the school are.
- Teach safety rules.
- Reward children who behave safely.
- Be prepared to punish children who are frequently reckless, (see *Discipline* for punishment strategies).
- Know the procedures for risk assessment in your school.
- Deal with accidents promptly. Make sure that you review what happened and take appropriate action to reduce the chance of a similar incident. Keep a written note, dated and signed.

On out-of-school activities:

- Undertake a preliminary visit that includes information you'll need for risk assessment that complies with school policy.
- Write a risk assessment and have this agreed with an appropriate member of staff.
- Inform parents in writing about the benefits and possible risks in the activity; obtain written permission from them.
- Prepare children for the out-of-school activity by including suitable health and safety rules in your teaching.
- Ensure that a suitable number of adults are available, who are able to accompany and take responsibility for the children.

- Make sure that all accompanying adults are aware of and will apply the rules that you have set.
- Review the health and safety aspects of activities as part of your evaluation of the event.
- If any incidents occur, make a signed record of the sequence of events as soon as possible.

Further reading

Websites often offer the most up-to-date information on safety issues. www.gov.uk/h_s_ev/ has general guidance on both educational visits and risk assessment as applies to England and Wales.

TTA Standards

3.1.3, 3.3.8.

Self-assessment by pupils

In many school policies on teaching and learning, one of the aims is to enable children to become independent learners. Self-evaluation is one of the strategies which will contribute to this goal. Children can use the process recommended in the first section of this book, just as well as adults. It is probably not appropriate to use the forms, as shown in the examples, but the thinking process is powerful. Pupils can ask the following questions about their work, behaviour, motivation, etc.:

'What do I want to improve?'
'What do I need to change?'
'What can I try out?'
'Did it work?'

This approach is closely aligned to the problem solving processes and cognitive acceleration strategies currently being promoted. It is a proactive approach and powerful mechanism for bringing about change.

When you ask a child to reflect on the quality of the work or behaviour he/she has produced, and he/she can respond by recognizing its worth and the need for improvement, the child has made a step towards his/her own decision making. Once children articulate what it is they are having difficulty with, they often seek help from peers and resolve the problem before it reaches the teacher.

Links

Active learning
Independent learning
Motivation
Part One
Target setting

Strategies

- Teach the steps of self-evaluation in appropriate classroom contexts.
- Allow pupils the opportunity to comment on their own work or behaviour.
- Encourage verbal/written reflection and suggested action.
- Allow pupils to target set in specific areas (e.g. learning tables, spelling, keeping a tidy desk, completing work).
- Introduce overt reflective discussion (possibly by showing how you carry it out).
- Allow children to seek peer help with problems.
- Get children to set targets and report back on them.

Development

One of the purposes of self-assessment is to reflect on what you know, but another part is to establish what you need to do. In truly proactive fashion, this will lead to target setting and further self-assessment. This would be a powerful learning tool if children could manage the process for themselves. Muschamp and a team of teachers in 1991 established a self-assessment system in a range of primary school classrooms. Her account, in Pollard (1996), indicates what a complex process this is if it is to be established as a school practice. First, the children have to be taught how to look at their work in a critical but constructive fashion. The early work of Muschamp's team revealed that children were not clear about the purpose of set work and the criteria by which it is judged. Beyond teaching the children to reflect on the correctness and quality of the work they then had to structure a procedure of discussion (teacher –

pupil, pupil – pupil) to enable successful target setting and self-assessment. By the end of a year they managed to tie this in to reporting to parents which involved contribution from the children.

Concept maps are used by some teachers as a way of getting children to brainstorm what they know about a topic. Concept maps, with the content filled in, can be a vehicle for setting targets, allowing children to see what they are expected to learn and identifying what they do not yet know.

Further reading

Muschamp, Y. (1996) 'Pupil self-assessment' in Pollard, A. (Ed.) *Readings for Reflective teaching in the Primary School*, London: Continuum.

TTA Standard

3.2.2.

Skills and strategies

Much emphasis is placed on what children should know, but it is just as important that children know how to do things. This is recognized quite clearly in subjects such as art and physical education. How to do things, (procedural knowledge) is just as important in other subjects too, for example, science, geography, English and even maths. When planning work for children it is important to have learning objectives which focus on developing skills and strategies. These might be practical skills, such as how to use a saw or a protractor, or they could be thinking skills such as how to get started on a problem or how to evaluate a product. Time spent teaching strategy will be well rewarded, as children will be able to transfer many of the skills and strategies to new situations.

In England certain skills have been identified as key skills which need to be developed. These are: communication, application of number, information technology, working with others, improving own learning and performance; and problem solving. Currently these are being examined in national qualifications in secondary schools (age 11–16 years). All formal post-16 education in England encompasses key skills. Secondary colleagues will be building on the strategies children have learned in primary schools.

Links

Communication about learning
Communicating clearly
Problem solving
Thinking skills

Strategies

- Identify and promote skills and strategies by making them the objective of the lesson.
- Monitor children's ability to apply their knowledge.
- Encourage discussions in class about how pupils worked things out and how they are going to carry out a task.

Further reading

Further information about key skills can be found on: www.atschool. edweb.co.uk/ufa/othersub.htm

Social development

Learning to be a social being is extremely important. Erickson (1963), a developmental psychologist, gives a framework for understanding personal human development, suggesting the stages that lead to self-sufficiency in adolescence. He suggests that there is a need for a safe and secure environment in order to develop trust. Part of social development is gaining concepts about gender, ethnicity, morality, citizenship and culture. Social interactions develop alongside intellectual, linguistic and physical capacities.

The milestones in social development are:

Babies take an interest in other babies at about 6 months, they smile and make noises at each other. By 12 months some turn-taking can be seen.

Between 12–24 months, infants play in *parallel*, that is they play alongside each other rather than together. They start to become aware of a world beyond themselves, engaging in the rules that govern social exchange, for example, turn-taking in conversation, expressing empathy, 'Mummy sad', 'Daddy cross'.

At 3 years *co-operative play* with turn-taking starts. When playing, the children start to know who to give in to and how to be in charge.

4 years sees *associative play* with sharing play items. *Theory of mind*, being able to understand the position of someone else, is acquired. Fighting is a normal development happening, though the cause of disputes is often soon forgotten.

6-year-olds have more friends and enemies and play in bigger groups; fights and feuds are sorted out with less adult help.

7–9-year-olds work out how to 'do friendship'; getting to know what they need to do to be accepted as peers.

In adolescence friends become as, or more, important than parents for social support. Girls tell their best girlfriends lots of things that their parents don't know. Often teenagers form large groups with a shared interest, e.g. music, football, clothes. Single-sex groups start to break down. Heterosexual couples become more common. By the end of adolescence each person often has a smaller group of both male and female friends.

The wider role of the teacher is clearly important in this aspect of child development. School provides a safe space outside the home where an understanding of the society can be explored. In your classroom some children need help in understanding their own behaviour, and that what they do affects others. You'll want to think about how you help to develop their ability to make and keep friends. The use of circle time is clearly one way to do this. The open discussion of issues, teaching children to be assertive rather than aggressive, is an important contribution.

Links

Discipline
Emotional development
Intellectual development
Relationships with pupils
Research and its uses

Further reading

Erickson, E. H. (1963) *Childhood and Society*, New York: Norton.
Meece, J. L. (1997) *Child and Adolescent Development for Educators*, New York: McGraw Hill. See pp. 323–6 for a succinct version of Erickson's theory.
Mosely, J. (1996) *Quality Circle Time*, Cambridge: LDA.
Mosely, J. (1999) *More Quality Circle Time*, Cambridge: LDA.

Keenan, T. (2002) *An Introduction to Child Development,* London: Sage. Chapter 9 Social Development is a useful introduction to some of the issues.

TTA Standard

2.4.

Special Educational Needs

You will be meeting the needs of *all* those who you teach. Some of the children in your classes will have *barriers to learning* (a key term in inclusion). These fall into a number of categories.

1. Anybody can have an off-day or two. From time to time there will be a slight dip in the way someone behaves or in the work done. Often these are just for a very short time and you will scarcely notice them. This is not a real cause for concern.
2. Then there are children with temporary Special Educational Needs (SEN). These temporary barriers may be a more than usual difficulty in learning to read, or spell, or remembering multiplication tables. Other temporary special needs may be an emotional barrier, caused by distress or illness or other causes. With appropriate teaching and support the temporary needs will pass and not remain a concern.
3. Children with more permanent barriers to learning need to have their special needs addressed throughout their schooling.

Meeting these needs, either those that will be ongoing or those that pass, presents a real challenge to teachers.

The *Special Needs Co-ordinator (SENCO)* is the person to ask about the children with SEN. This is a key member of staff with specific information, resources and, most importantly, extra knowledge to help you to plan and deliver appropriate teaching.

In your class you'll be the one to spot any children who are not making the progress you'd expect for their age and developmental stage. Schooling makes demands on children that home and community may not. For example, children have to be co-operative members of the class in order to learn and they have to stick at tasks that demand attention. You may find children in your class who, for example, cannot do the work that others can, are really unco-operative rather than occasionally difficult, or have a very short attention span. This may mean that these children have special needs. Should you be correct in your assessment, either about academic achievement or behaviour, your concern will trigger the events that are needed for School Action (SA) (see *Code of Practice* for this and other SEN terms). Your school will have a procedure for you to follow to get things moving.

If you teach in an early years' setting your knowledge about developmental milestones will assist in the judgements that you make about children's progress. You will be one of the first people outside the home to see the child in an educational setting. You could be the one to first suspect and identify some of the following. For example:

Sight problems – learning to read requires a child to be able to focus at 60 cm or less. You'll look for things such as the child reading better from the big book than the individual reader, or writing with the nose pressed to the page.

Hearing problems – intermittent deafness or 'glue ear' is common in children with persistent bad colds.

Emotional and behavioural difficulties – a child with an excessive emotional response to simple requests that you make.

If the cause for concern is confirmed, Early Years Action (EYA) will be invoked.

EYA/SA means that extra differentiation of the learning tasks that you set is needed. It means that you have to offer additional support for the child with SEN. The action will be set out in an *Individual Education Plan (IEP)*. Children with an IEP in EYA/SA will be reliant on you to provide appropriate differentiated teaching for their needs. Some children come into primary school with an IEP which will identify short-term targets, which are *different from*, or *additional* to those you'll set for the rest of the class. The IEP is an important tool. The targets in the IEP should be SMART:

Specific to the needs of each child
Measurable
Achievable
Realistic and
Time limited

Most schools use a simple format for IEPs. Often a software package is used to write them. The IEP should supply the information you require to help you. You need to use children's records to find out what they *can do* and what they *already know*. Use this information, with the IEP targets, to differentiate further the work you set. For example, a child who finds literacy difficult, needs small steps in learning and takes a long time to understand what you are teaching, may need you to:

rewrite worksheets using short sentences and non-technical words (even then you may need someone to read it to the child);

break tasks into small steps and give each of the steps out one at a time;

allow extra learning time for key concepts by setting the rest of your children more complex and demanding tasks.

Take the time to differentiate the work you set and the ways in which you teach. Once you have successful tasks and materials make these reusable, rather than throw away, resources. Keep your successful teaching strategies, drop those that aren't helpful.

You will be writing and contributing to the writing of IEPs for the children with SEN in your class. Your knowledge about the children in your class is very, very important, and will assist you setting targets, thinking about the way these should be taught, how this is to be managed, and about monitoring progress.

When a child in your class has newly identified needs, often the head or the SENCO will conduct the first interviews with the child and the parents. Your responsibility as the class teacher will be to follow up on this by helping the child to realize how to make progress. You'll be expected to assist in keeping parents informed by reports that you write and at meetings which you have with them. You'll be given support to do this.

Some children with SEN will have *learning assistants* (sometimes called classroom assistants) to help them. It is still your job to differentiate the learning and the teaching, to design and set the tasks. The learning assistant may be able to help you to do this more effectively because of their knowledge about and experience with the child. They may know about and select additional resources and generally make your learning outcomes realistic and achievable. Usually the children they support have exceptionally severe and often permanent learning difficulties. These may include intel-lectual impairment sometimes in combination with sensory or physical impairment. This may include sight, hearing and/or mobility difficulties.

Some children may have sensory or physical impairments which do not impede their learning ability, and they may have a classroom assistant to help overcome the difficulty. You will be expected to take their needs into account in your teaching and to use the classroom assistant to do this. For example:

A child with a sight impairment may need a print size of 24 or even 32 point, plus a strong electric light, to undertake the worksheet you are setting for the most able children in the class. The classroom assistant needs the worksheet in good time in order to prepare it.

A child with a hearing impairment may need you to use an amplifier so that your speech can be heard. The classroom assistant will check that the child can hear you.

Wheelchair users often require more space. The classroom assistant will help you to organize the rest of the class to give the space.

Use any extra help you can get. Ideally, this will be an efficient and experienced learning assistant, but don't rule out volunteers. Older children working with younger children, peer support, community helpers, all are tried and tested, and, given the right set of circumstances, they work. Remember that parents can often support their own child and do so willingly and well.

The need to deal effectively with children with *emotional and behavioural difficulties* (EBD) is becoming more important. These children will have IEPs with short-term targets for behaviour, sometimes referred to as an Individual Behaviour Plan (IBP). This is often in the form of an agreed contract between the child and the teachers. The contract will start with an area where you and the child think progress can be made. It will set out exactly what the child needs to do in specific contexts, for example, the child is required to start on work as soon as it is set and to finish a specified amount of work each day. There may be 'time out' strategies for when the child feels that he/she may be about to lose control. The child may go, with your permission, to another class for five minutes.

On the occasions when things go seriously wrong for the child with EBD, there should be an agreed system for getting additional support into the class quickly and without fuss. You may not leave the class, so send a reliable pupil or two to fetch another teacher. The support should be from a senior member of staff: you'll need support from more experienced staff to meet some challenging behaviours. Children with severe and persistent difficulties may get extra help from a learning assistant.

The aim is always to keep focusing on achievable targets for the child. It is not the child but the acts that the child carries out which are offensive and unacceptable. It is the behaviour that can be changed. You'll need to use a graduated response to children with EBD. Recognize that they may need much more positive reinforcement than other children. You always need to have one more step in your repertoire to deal effectively with children with EBD.

Common terms and learning difficulties

These are some of the terms you may need to know. This list is by no means complete. Your SENCO will help you with the less common and the more esoteric conditions that some children have. The 'health warning' is that it is not possible to generalize from the named conditions, the ways in which this will affect the individual child. Each child experiences and overcomes difficulties in his/her own way. Whilst your SENCO will suggest ways that often work for many children, don't expect these to be foolproof. You and your colleagues may have to work hard sometimes to spot what works for a particular child. It is a great feeling when this happens.

AD(H)D *Attention Deficit (Hyperactivity) Disorder*   Usually there are three areas of behaviour – inattentiveness, implusivity and overactivity – that are barriers to learning. Some of these children need highly structured programmes to make progress in school. Each child with ADD will have an individual pattern of behaviour with different 'triggers' and responses dependent on a range of things – who the teacher is, the subject, the time of day, what happened just before the lesson, e.g. an exciting playtime, etc.

MLD *Mild learning difficulties/moderate learning difficulties* There are a wide range of these. Many children may have difficulty with one or all the key skills. Some can learn well but they may need much more time and help than others in the same class. Others may have organizational difficulties, things like often being late, frequently with the wrong pieces of kit, and getting lost. Many children develop excellent coping strategies and should be expected to develop into successful learners.

SLD *Specific Learning Difficulties (including dyslexia)*   Some or all of the following may be seen in some children: difficulty in sequencing, difficulty with spelling, difficulty in remembering a sequence of sounds in words, difficulty in recall of item and number sequences, and poor handwriting. Usually, if well taught, these children will find learning paths and develop strategies that compensate for these barriers to learning.

Asperger's Syndrome   This is part of the spectrum that is called autism. Pupils with this can do very well in school settings with appropriate support. In primary school they may have delayed speech, cognitive difficulties, problems with understanding and using social cues, and an absorbing interest. Over time some of these improve, especially where help is given to the child to develop coping strategies.

Dyspraxia   Often described as clumsy, these children have difficulties in planning and carrying out skilled, non-habitual motor tasks in a correct sequence. It is sensible to allow children with dyspraxia extra time to complete tasks. They often need structured support with many motor tasks.

Links

Code of Practice
Differentiation
Inclusion
Learning styles
Monitoring and assessment strategies
Recording individual progress
Research and its uses
Teaching in teams
Working with other adults

Strategies

How would you provide proof for 'yes' answers to these questions? Turn these into statements to use as strategies or targets.

- Do I make sure that all the children in my class take part in all subjects and all activities?
- Do I plan lessons to include all children's needs?
- Do all the children take part in all the lessons?

- Do I use different learning styles and teaching approaches? Do I for example, experiment with ways of presenting things that don't need much skill in reading?
- Do tasks and activities allow different children to get to different outcomes?
- Do I allow children with SEN the extra time they need to learn the facts and knowledge needed, by setting other children more complex and demanding tasks? (But not tasks that require new facts or knowledge otherwise children with SEN never catch up.)
- Are all children encouraged both to reflect on their own ways of learning and assess what they have learned?
- Do I make sensible use of learning support staff, involving them in planning and preparation for the child?
- Are other adults encouraged to work with the children in my class?
- Do we celebrate the successes we have?
- Do I enjoy the challenge that children with SEN present?

Development

Other countries have their own policies about SEN. Some segregate children with SEN into specialized schools. This is what used to happen in England and Wales. Recently though, inclusion is on the agenda for schools. Whilst inclusion is not just about SEN, it is true that it is by far the largest area of concern for teachers, parents and policy makers. The policy was made explicit in 1997 in a DfEE consultation document *Excellence for all Children: Meeting Special Educational Needs.* This was used as an opportunity to review aspects of the education of children and young people with barriers to learning. The key principles of early identification and appropriate intervention were made policy. It was a major review of principles established by the Warnock Report (DES, 1978) and included a revision of the Code of Practice (DfES, 2001a). The policy means that the number of children with SEN to be included in mainstream schooling is likely to increase. See the entry on the *Code of Practice* (CoP) for England to gain an overview on policy and practice.

Children with SEN are often a cause of anxiety for teachers. They worry about their ability to meet the needs of *all* the children they teach and how they will cope with the extra demand made by children with SEN. Fortunately, there is a wealth of information and experience on how to do this. In school, the SENCO can often help

you to manage the teaching and learning so that children with SEN
are not a burden. There are excellent books, websites and courses
for teachers. What is true is that children with SEN are often key in
making each of us more effective teachers for all our pupils. They
are the children who teach us how to teach. Meeting their special
needs makes us think hard about teaching and learning. This makes
us more aware of how we might teach concepts, facts, skills,
knowledge, ideas and values to *all* children. You may find that
children with SEN are particularly rewarding to teach. If this is the
case then developing this aspect of your career is something you
should consider.

Further reading

There are a great many books and websites and organizations with useful
information on SEN as a whole and on most of the conditions associated
with particular special needs. The following is a short list:

Benton, P. and O'Brien, T. (Eds) (2000) *Special Needs and the Beginning
Teacher*, London: Continuum.
Carpenter, B., Ashdown, R. and Bovair, K. (Eds) (2001) *Enabling Access:
Effective Learning for Pupils with Learning Difficulties*, 2nd edn, London:
David Fulton.
Department for Education and Employment (DfEE) (1997) *Excellence for all
Children, Meeting Special Educational Needs*, London: DfEE.
Department of Education and Science (DES) (1978) *Report on the
Commission on Special Education*, London: HMSO (Warnock Report).
Department for Education and Skills (DfES) (2001a) *Special Needs Code of
Practice* (DfES 581/2001), London: DfES.
Department for Education and Skills (DfES) (2001b) *Schools Achieving
Success*, London: HMSO.
Farrell, M. (2000) *The Special Education Handbook*, 2nd edn, London:
David Fulton.
Flavell, E. (2001) *Preparing to Include Special Children in Mainstream
Schools, A Practical Guide*, London: David Fulton.
Garner, P. and Dwyfor Davies, J. (2001) *Introducing Special Educational
Needs: A Companion Guide for Student Teachers*, London: David Fulton.
Wearmouth, J. (Ed.) (2001) *Special Educational Provision in the Context of
Inclusion: Policy and Practice in Schools*, London: David Fulton/Open
University.
Websites (note that there are many more than these.)
See DfES webpages for the most up-to-date information about SEN
http//:inclusion.ngfl.gov.uk
www.halcyon.com/marcs/sped.html   North American site with many use-
ful links.

www.ipsea.org.uk   Independent advice for parents.
www.nasen.org.uk   National Association of Special Educational Needs.

TTA Standards

2.6, 3.2.4, 3.3.4.

Standardized tests

These are tests which have been trialled and matched to a norm. Like IQ (Intelligence Quotient) the norm is 100 and children's results are converted using a table. The table allows for the age of the child to be taken into account. The child does the test which is marked and a 'raw' score is generated. This is then 'converted' using a table to a 'standardized score'. If a younger child gains the same raw score as an older child, the younger child will get a higher standardized score. When scores or ages lie on the limits of the normal range, the test is considered to be a less reliable predictor of ability. Standardized tests can be used to compare groups in various locations as well as measuring the child against the norm in different years.

Links

Research and its uses
Summative assessment

Development

A standardized test can be useful in research because it gives a norm which can be used to establish a base line and then children can be re-tested with the knowledge that a similar test will give comparable results.

However, Croll (1996) offers a nice comparison between norm referenced and the criterion referenced assessments which have come into more common use for measuring children's performance. He indicates that it may not be easy to operate a pure criterion referenced system when we have age-related expectations. Certainly, in the light of his comments, it is worth reflecting on how a criterion referenced system is actually used in the National Curriculum (DfEE, 2000).

Going a step further, Lindsay (1996), reviews the place of standardized IQ tests in school in the light of children's, the school's and society's needs.

Further reading

Croll, P. (1996) 'Norm and criterion referenced assessment', in Pollard, A. (Ed.) *Readings for Reflective Teaching in the Primary School*, London: Continuum.

Department for Education and Employment (DfEE) (2000) *The National Curriculum: Handbook for Primary Teachers in England Key Stages 1 and 2*, London: DfEE/QCA (www.nc.uk.net).

Lindsay, G. (1996) 'Assessment of the primary school child', in Pollard, A. (Ed.) *Readings for Reflective Teaching in the Primary School*, London: Continuum.

QCA site has information about key stage tests at www.qca.org.uk/ca/tests

TTA Standard

3.2.3.

Subject knowledge

In teaching you need a good knowledge of the subjects you are going to teach plus a knowledge of how to teach them (pedagogic knowledge). For example, knowing numbers to 10 is something we all know but once young children have learned the counting rhyme, 1, 2, 3, 4, 5, 6, 7, 8, 9, 10, what else do they need to know? They need to know about conservation of quantity, recognize the symbol, count using one-to-one correspondence, be able to name how many are in a set and know which numbers come before and after others. These are all aspects of knowing numbers to 10 and they all need to be taught. As a teacher there is a significant shift to be made from having personal knowledge to having words to successfully teach that knowledge and finding tasks to help children understand that knowledge.

If you are confident and knowledgeable about subjects you will provide correct information to pupils and you will be able to answer their questions. You will also convey a sense of structure and continuity in the work that you do with the children. You will be in a better position to challenge children's thinking and will be able to resolve their misconceptions. Enthusiasm for a subject is easily conveyed to children. Unfortunately the opposite can be true too.

There are some subjects which will be your strengths and the children you teach will benefit from your expertise. In the subjects where you are not so knowledgeable you will need to research the topics and prepare your medium- and short-term planning carefully. Within a school's staff you will often be able to find someone (such as the co-ordinator) who will be able to provide some support for your weaker subjects.

Links

Active learning
Independent learning
Medium-term planning
Research and its uses

Strategies

- Research areas you are not sure of so that you provide an accurate and true experience for children.
- Convey enthusiasm.
- Seek guidance when you need it.
- Inform yourself well on topics as you teach them.
- Find opportunities, such as courses and conferences, to strengthen your teaching.

Development

A depth of subject knowledge and a particular interest in a subject will enhance your teaching and will often prove a strong motivator for the children. Spontaneous questions will elicit knowledgeable responses from you. You may even provide additional and interesting explanations which you, from your knowledge base, see as connected information; things which another teacher will be unaware of. This allows you to extend children's thinking and is particularly stimulating for able children.

Teachers who have a good knowledge base in a subject are more likely to be relaxed about teaching the subject, enthusiastic about the subject and less likely to teach misconceptions.

Further reading

TTA see *Handbook of Guidance on QTS Standards and ITT Requirements* which can be found on www.canteach.gov.uk/community/ itt/requirements/handbook

TTA website has useful information: www.canteach.gov.uk

TTA Standard

2.1.

Summative assessment

Summative assessments are those that are made to summarize performance. They tend to mark stages of progress through the education system. The main purpose of summative assessment is to identify the stage a child has reached at that point in time. Where marked papers are returned, these may be used for formative assessment. English national tests' results are analysed and the results are sent to schools to inform about weaknesses in particular topics. Analysis of individual papers can indicate a child's areas of difficulty. Typical summative assessments are GCSE exams, key stage test results and GNVQ which are all national assessments. The key stage tests are analysed and a report is made on national performance. In this way summative assessment can be used in a formative way.

Within school, summative assessment might take the form of half-termly and end-of-year tests, end of topic assessments, end of year records to pass on to the next teacher, reports to parents, or records of achievement.

Links

Baseline assessment
Formative assessment
Recording individual progress

Strategies

- Ensure ongoing records are kept which will inform you when you need to summarize a pupil's achievements.
- Provide an assessment to summarize what a pupil understands about a topic at this point in time.
- Consider the use of self-evaluation when judging what a pupil knows or does not know.
- Be familiar with national assessment requirements.

Development

Assessment is used for many different purposes and therefore it is important that you select a form of assessment which provides you with the information you need. For a good summary of the purposes and principles of assessment refer to Harlen *et al.* (1996) p. 264.

Further reading

Harlen, W., Gipps, C., Broadfoot, P. and Nuttall, D. (1996) 'Assessment purposes and principles', in Pollard, A. (Ed.) *Readings for Reflective Teaching in the Primary School*, London, Continuum.
QCA website has test information: www.qca.org.uk/ca/tests

TTA Standards

3.2.2, 3.2.3.

Target setting

The purpose of target setting is to have clear goals which focus learning. There are several layers of target setting occurring in school. The teacher will have targets for whole class learning and for individuals (learning objectives). Target setting for pupils could be part of a pupil self-evaluation system. Some target setting for pupils is shared with parents. It is particularly important that achievement of these targets is recognized. This can be difficult to organize at the end of the school year.

Target setting for the teacher is part of your self-evaluation system and continuing professional development. A more formal target setting for teachers can be met when participating in an appraisal system. Here the targets are usually set for a whole year.

Schools have targets too. These are shown in the School Development Plan. Many LEAs set schools targets to achieve in key stage tests. These are usually projections of baseline assessment or previous Key Stage results. These targets are part of the drive to raise standards in schools throughout the country (England). Inspections can result in 'actionable' comments which then become school targets.

Links

Active learning
Baseline assessment

Continuing professional development
Monitoring pupils' learning
Summative assessment
Teachers' employment and conditions

Strategies

- Set clear objectives in long-, medium- and short-term planning and monitor pupils' achievement of them.
- Create time to set targets with individuals and time to follow them up.
- Encourage children to evaluate what they have done and what they need to do next.
- Be aware of national and local target setting for your school. Match these to your class performance.
- Set targets for yourself about your teaching skills.

Development

Target setting systems are time consuming to maintain, especially when targets are individualized. However, individual targets are an effective way of meeting the needs of individual pupils. As much of the work will take place in the child's own time, with individual targets it is worth getting the co-operation of the child in setting the target. They will also need to know how they can go about achieving the target. A well-known acronym for target setting is SMART which stands for, **S**pecific, **M**easurable, **A**greed, **R**ealistic, **T**ime, all qualities which good target setting should include.

Muschamp (1991) provides a powerful account of setting up self-assessment and target setting (see *Self-assessment*). It was clearly a worthwhile approach for the children involved. Her teachers felt that there were links between self-selected targets and becoming an independent learner.

Smith (2001) describes a process for successfully establishing target setting. His five steps are: timelines, future-basing, templates, anchoring and affirmations.

A fundamental issue when running a target setting system is to establish how you will monitor that the targets have been achieved. This needs planning into your medium- and short-term strategies. If you do not follow up the target setting, the motivation will die and the system become non-effective. No matter how independently a child is able to work, you are part of the contract which is made when the target is set.

Further reading

Muschamp, Y. (1991) 'Pupil self-assessment' in Pollard, A. (Ed.) *Readings for Reflective Teaching in the Primary School*, London: Continuum.

Smith, A. (2001) 'The strategies to accelerate learning in the classroom' in Banks, F. and Shelton Mayes, A. (Eds) *Early Professional Development for Teachers*, London: David Fulton/Open University.

TTA Standard

3.1.

Teachers' employment and conditions

In England and Wales these are reviewed annually. The pay structure is fixed by law. However, whilst there is some automatic annual progression, increasingly your employers, the governors, have scope for discretion. The school will have a policy document about pay and conditions. Your job description will say what your school expects from you, and should be reviewed and updated regularly. It will state both the generic roles you'll be expected to undertake and any specific tasks that are your responsibility. In England teachers work 195 days a year, five of these are training days. Hours are also specified, but there is a let-out clause on this, as you have 'to discharge effectively your professional duties'. This means that most teachers work much more than a 36-hour week. Professional duties include teaching, preparation for teaching, marking and report writing. Who you will teach and which room you will teach in, will be decided by your line manager, who is often the head teacher.

Performance management means that you will continue to be a life-long learner. You will be developing the professional portfolio you started pre qualification. As a newly qualified teacher (NQT) you'll start your first post with some targets. As there is always something more to understand as a teacher, targets will not be hard to find. Furthermore, in most education systems, the extra experience gained, will boost income. This aspect of your career is managed over a two-year cycle.

Your work is under scrutiny all the time. At first this seems intimidating but you will soon become used to it. The results you get and how you teach will be inspected regularly. These judgements will be used in different ways, one of which is to plan for your development. In addition to the appraisal you get from your colleagues, there are local inspectors and the Office for Standards in Education (Ofsted) inspectors, who visit schools as part of the local and national accountability and quality system for England. Judgements made about your work contribute to the judgement made about the school.

Links
Continuing professional development (CPD)
Discipline
Expectations about pupils' learning
Research and its uses
Safety
Teaching in teams
Values and ethos
Working with other adults

Strategies
- Be ambitious about all those you teach – expect them to do well and to achieve.
- Be aware of the expectations your colleagues have about you, know what your professional responsibilities are and undertake these wholeheartedly.
- Before accepting employment check that the pay and conditions are what you want, including arrangements for your support and further opportunities for CPD.
- Prepare thoroughly for all aspects of performance review.
- Set realistic targets for your own development, these should take account of those the school has as its focus.
- Choose CPD activities that can be used to develop your curriculum vitae (CV).

Development
Beyond pay and conditions you'll want to understand what teaching involves. An important part of your professional responsibilities is the expectations you have about pupils. As a teacher you are expected to want your pupils to do as well as they

possibly can. This means that you won't accept anything less than the best from everyone. Their 'best' means working towards raising achievement in all aspects of learning. But it also means that you have to do this from a knowledge base that respects and deals with difference. How you treat your pupils and work with colleagues, support workers, parents and everyone else will demonstrate your understanding of your responsibilities. You are expected to evaluate yourself as a teacher, to build on your strengths and to improve on any weaknesses. You'll work within the rules that are laid down by statute. This is a great deal to take on. It doesn't all have to be learned at once but it does all have to be learned.

Further reading

Bubb, S. and Hoare, P. (2001) *Performance Management: Monitoring Teaching in the Primary School*, London: David Fulton.
A comprehensive guide.
Cowley, S. (1999) *Starting Teaching: How to Succeed and Survive*, London: Cassell, Part IV is about teachers' employment.
Moyles, J. and Robinson, G. (Eds) (2002) *Beginning Teaching: Beginning Learning in Primary Education*, 2nd edn, Buckingham: Open University.
www.teachernet.gov.uk has the most up-to-date information about employment for teachers in England.
www.canteach.gov.uk has useful links.

TTA Standard
1.8.

Teaching in teams

You are responsible for working with your teacher colleagues, who will expect you to share responsibility for the school curriculum in all sorts of ways. They will expect a professional commitment to joint planning and preparation. At first you will need colleagues' help to overcome some of the barriers to learning that some of the children in your class may have. More experienced colleagues will support target setting for children who are very able. Your subject expertise means that colleagues expect you to take a lead working towards solutions for the school in this area of the curriculum. You have responsibilities for the welfare of the children in your class. You will be expected to report on anything you think is amiss. You will want to celebrate children's successes, sharing these with colleagues. In a leadership role you will be working with some other adults in school, e.g. nursery staff, classroom assistants, and volunteers, right from the start. You will become aware of the issues that face the school as a whole. The management group of more senior teachers will expect your support and understanding.

Links

Communication with parents
Continuing professional development (CPD)
Teachers' employment and conditions
Working with other adults

Strategies

As a colleague

- Know your personal qualities, work from your strengths, but address your weaknesses.
- Be prepared to be flexible; it's supportive to release your classroom assistant on occasions to help in another class, it's a help to take a few extra children sometimes, it's ok to change your mind when there is new information.
- Empathy – putting yourself in someone else's position, under-standing not just the words but the emotions that lie underneath – is a real strength. In the staff room, at year group meetings, listen to what is meant not just what is said.
- Be task involved. Judge yourself and others on what is done not by who does it. It is about doing your best and doing an honest job.
- Be assertive. For example, find a form of words to tell someone why you are annoyed, 'When you do ..., I find there is a problem. Can we find a way to deal with this?'.
- Accept thanks graciously.
- Keep a hold on your sense of humour. There are times when humour can really help, but not always!
- Develop your understanding of the structures within which your school works, how it is governed, the challenges and the plan that has been agreed with the governors to meet these.
- Attend meetings and read the notes that are sent round and the e-mails (even when these seem, at first, to make little sense).

- Listen, ask questions, take part in the staffroom banter and conversations. It is tempting to stay in your own classroom when you have a great deal to do but, if you want to really be a part of the school, get into the staffroom, get yourself known and get to know colleagues. Beware though, of the staffroom cynics, often they are very attractive company, witty and sharp but their comments can lower morale.

Development

Being part of a team means that you will get support in your day to day work and in career planning. Your colleagues will suggest when you should take on additional responsibility. Fairly soon, perhaps in your second year as a teacher, you will want to think about this. A curriculum responsibility, or other leadership role within your school, is often the first move. Think too about a wider role, working with parents and volunteers or being the teacher representative on the Governing Body or moving into union or professional association work. Moving school to gain experience with a different team is another decision that you will want to make at some point.

Further reading

Cowley, S. (1999) *Starting Teaching: How to Succeed and Survive*, London: Continuum.

Thody, A., Gray, B. and Bowden, D. (2000) *The Teacher's Survival Guide*, London: Continuum.

TTA Standards

1.5, 1.6, 3.1.4, 3.3.13.

Thinking skills (including cognitive acceleration)

As technology develops the needs of society are changing and access to information is easier. This has brought about a subtle change in education. The need now is to educate people to manage the new technologies, to be able to solve problems and make decisions. This has tipped the balance of skills and knowledge slightly more in the direction of skills, particularly problem solving and thinking skills. Also, in the effort to raise standards of pupil achievement in education, people are examining the ways in which children learn effectively, hoping this will unlock the door to learning. Research into thinking and cognitive acceleration is currently being utilized to create better learning environments for children. What is particularly exciting is that this work, once the domain of psychologists, is now being linked to practical classroom strategies with interesting results (Adey, 1988; Adhami *et al.*, 1997; Smith, 2001).

Links

Able children
Active learning
Independent learning
Problem solving
Learning styles
Questioning
Target setting

Strategies

- Discuss with children how they will go about a task.
- Promote problem solving strategies.
- Get children to set targets.
- Make sure children are aware and understand the learning objective and how it is to be achieved.
- Get children to reflect on the mental strategies that they are using.
- Encourage articulation of how they are working things out.

Development

Reflecting on the way we think ourselves is often termed metacognition. Thinking skills have long been a subject for study but two recent research projects at King's College, London University, are generating much interest. These are *Cognitive Acceleration in Science Education* (CASE) (Adey, 1988) and *Cognitive Acceleration in Mathematics Education* (CAME) (Adhami *et al.*, 1997). Cognitive acceleration is a term used to describe a process which allows children to speed up their ability to learn. By teaching children to understand the way they work and to develop strategies for solving problems, it is believed that children can learn more effectively and perform to a higher level. Results from both CASE and CAME, which are based on Piagetian problem solving, have been very promising in showing improvement and are transfering to other subjects. Other projects, where students employ metacognitive techniques, are also currently popular. These techniques require the student to consciously consider what processes and strategies they are using when working at a task.

Smith (2001) discusses 'pole-bridging' which is about utilizing as much of the brain as possible when doing a task. This can be done by articulating aloud what you are doing as you do it (talk yourself through, take notes, reflect and hypothesize on the situation). The plenary of a lesson often involves a form of reflection on the lesson. Smith goes on to discuss recent research on how our brains work and how we can maximize the learning environment of the classroom by utilizing this knowledge.

Further reading

Adey, P. (1988) 'Cognitive acceleration: review and prospects', *International Journal of Science Education*, 10: 2, 121–34.

Adhami, M., Johnson, D. and Shayer, M. (1997) 'Does "CAME" work?', Summary report on phase 2 of the cognitive acceleration in mathematics education, CAME, project in *Proceedings of the Day Conference of the British Society for Research into Learning Mathematics*, Bristol, November 1997.

Smith, A. (2001) 'What the most recent brain research tells us about learning' in Banks, F. and Shelton Mayes, A. (Eds) *Early Professional Development for Teachers*, London: David Fulton/Open University.

TTA Standard

3.2.5.

Time management

Teaching is a demanding profession so it is very important that you manage your time well and as efficiently as possible. Not only do you need good time management for yourself but you also need to expect it from your pupils. As a teacher, it is very easy to take on more than you can possibly manage. It is better to give a polite but firm refusal when approached, than agree and then not have time to do the job well. Work out your limitations and stick to them. This is good time management and avoids you and everyone else getting stressed. On the same theme, it is important to create your own free space, away from school work. This should be a point in the evening when you stop work and a regular commitment to a leisure time activity.

One of the classic ways to manage time effectively is to get started promptly and to limit the time to achieve tasks. If, on the other hand, you give yourself an open-ended schedule you will probably use up all of your time.

Try to avoid duplication when writing planning documents. Use key words and bullet points in your planning. Plan ahead as much as possible so that you can have part of each day to yourself. Use previous plans and ideas from text books if they are appropriate. ICT systems are useful here. Try to be efficient in your record keeping too. Decide for what purposes you need to keep records and then select the relevant information. Have a system which culminates in useful information at the end of the year.

Much of the above applies to organizing the children in your class. They too need to learn good time management habits, such as getting started promptly on tasks and knowing how long they have to expected completion. Make these expectations overt so that they learn to develop their work habits. Allow children to make judgements about work. For example, 'How long do you think you need to complete this?' and, 'How are you going to start this problem?'. Children also appreciate reward for work well done and well managed. This might be stars, house points, treats, a chance of a free choice activity, extra playtime, etc.

Links

Completed work
Expectations about pupils' learning
Independent learning
Long-term planning
Medium-term planning
Rewards
Teaching in teams
Working with other adults

Strategies

- Make overt references to starting and completing work (expectations).
- Plan as far ahead as possible.
- Allow personal space in each day.
- Reward yourself and pupils for work well managed.

Development

Pollard *et al.* (1994) in their research on how pupils spend their time in the primary classroom, found that they were 'task engaged', organizing or waiting for the teacher 20 per cent of the time and distracted for 20 per cent of the time. Looked at another way, most primary children spent between 65–75 per cent of their time on task and task related activity. The question the researchers were left with was, 'Whether this "on task" activity is educationally productive?'.

Further reading

Pollard, A., Broadfoot, P., Croll, P., Osborn, M. and Abbott, D. (1994) 'Using classroom time' in Pollard, A. (Ed.) *Readings for Reflective Teaching in the Primary School*, London: Continuum.

TTA Standard

3.3.7.

Timing within lessons

Timing of a lesson is a blend of planning the right length tasks, teaching within your allotted time slot, having a sense of time passing during the lesson and switching or staying with tasks depending on whether the children are engaged in a task or not.

If you check the clock at regular intervals you will build up an awareness of the time passing. At the end of the lesson you can evaluate whether you remained on schedule or not. This depends on you estimating, then writing on your lesson plan, how much time you anticipate using for each part of the lesson. You will begin to refine your medium-term planning to match the pace of the children you are teaching. Increasingly you will find that you are able to judge how long tasks will take and the level of the work that engages the children.

Do not be afraid to alter the timing of a lesson if things are going well or badly. It is best to move on if the children are restless and finding it difficult to pay attention. (Windy days, Friday afternoons and school entertainments are some of the 'attention challenges'!) It is also your decision to extend a piece of work if you think the children are having a meaningful learning experience.

Regularly running out of time alters the balance of the lesson and means the conclusion is neglected. This is a valuable part of the lesson which gives you an opportunity to re-focus children's attention on the learning objective(s). You also need to maintain a balance between listening and doing. Overly long introductions leave little time for children to practise and consolidate the ideas and thus remember them.

Links

Lesson plan structure
Pace
Time management

Strategies

- Review timing of tasks and adapt medium- and short-term planning.
- Enter anticipated length of teaching and tasks on your lesson plan.
- Ensure that all sections of a lesson are delivered.
- Consider the balance within the lesson between listening, responding and doing tasks.

TTA Standard

3.3.7.

Transitions

Transitions are the parts of the lesson when pupils are moving from one activity to the next. This could be when the whole class are required to enter or leave the room, when they move to and from the carpet session to their plenary or group work, or when they individually finish a piece of work and are required to move to the next task. All these situations have the potential for some pupils to behave poorly and not get engaged in the next task. You need to be well organized, clear in your expectations and clear in your instructions, so that the pupils have no doubt what is expected of them. If they know what they are supposed to be doing this makes it easier to deal with situations where they are not following instructions, because they clearly know they are in the wrong. Classes and children will vary in their ability to move round the room with control. Ultimately you are aiming for an environment where pupils can move round the room in an orderly and purposeful manner without you 'policing the traffic'. This form of self-discipline needs to be encouraged and praised and opportunities offered for it to occur. In the beginning though, there will be a need to establish discipline, which needs to come through you.

When clearing away, have a specific location for pupils to go when finished. You may need to do more than this. For example, it is not enough to say, 'go to the carpet when you have cleared away your art things'. This clearing up could spread over a long period of time and the early finishers will get bored sitting on the carpet if there is nothing to do. Often children will hurry if they think they are missing some new activity, so you might read a story or set a puzzle whilst the last of the artists complete their task.

Links

Discipline
Explaining
Instruction
Timing within lessons

Strategies

- Ensure that pupils enter and leave the room in an orderly fashion.
- Make your expectations clear about where pupils should be at the start and finish of a task before allowing them to move away from the previous situation.
- Ensure resources are laid out or available prior to the lesson.
- Plan good extension tasks for the fast finishers.
- If pupils are going to finish at different times make sure that they know what they are to do as and when they finish.
- Be prepared to start another activity which late finishers can join in when they complete their last task.
- If the class cannot move properly all at once, send them to tasks a group at a time.

Development

Initially managing transitions is about you having control of the class and creating an orderly environment, but it should develop from there into a situation where children want their classroom to have an atmosphere where they move around like purposeful adults and engage in tasks because they are meaningful. It should not be a place where they have to keep one eye on the teacher to see if he/she is watching them and feel they have to misbehave because the teacher's attention is elsewhere. You will be working towards self-discipline. You should be able to move towards this by giving the pupils, who are capable, more opportunities to manage their work. On occasions peer pressure can be used in group tasks to get the pupils with less self-discipline to toe the line. Croll and Hastings (1996) and Moyles (1995) promote the establishment of rules in the classroom. Laslett and Smith (1998) are more direct in giving four rules of classroom management.

Further reading

Croll, P. and Hastings, N. (1996) *Effective Primary Teaching*, London: David Fulton.

Moyles, J. (1995) 'The classroom as a teaching and learning context' in Moyles, J. (Ed.) *Beginning Teaching, Beginning Learning*, Buckingham: Open University.

Moyles, J. and Robinson, G. (Eds) (2002) *Beginning Teaching: Beginning Learning in Primary Education*, 2nd edn, Buckingham: Open University.

Laslett, R. and Smith, C. (1998) 'Four rules of class management' in Pollard, A. (Ed.) *Readings for Reflective Teaching in the Primary School*, London: Continuum.

Values and ethos

Your values will be reflected in your professional role. You'll want all those you teach to succeed at the highest level. To do this you have to know and understand about yourself, those who you teach and the education system in which you work. This is a tall order, so start by examining your own values. What do you hold dear? How does this square with what the society in which you live expects from you? For example, if you think honesty is important how does this match expectations of your family, community and the schools that you know? Being honest is not absolute; in part it is about knowing when to tell the truth and when it is right to keep silent. Moral judgements are not always easy to make, sometimes you just have to hope that you're doing the 'right thing'. What you do and say, in any given situation, will establish your values with the children. For example, a pupil who disrupts a lesson by throwing paint on the floor might be punished, but a child who accidentally spills paint would not. The distinctive atmosphere of justice and equity you establish will be recognized as your values in action and the ethos of your classroom.

Links

Bullying
Culture
Discipline
Emotional development
Equal opportunities
Ethnicity
Expectations about pupils' learning
Parents
Purposeful working atmosphere
Relationships with pupils
Research and its uses
Social development
Teachers' employment and conditions

Strategies

Some principles to support the strategies you use:

- Know the range of social and emotional development that you're likely to meet with your pupils.
- Accept that you need to develop your pupils' sense about right and wrong.
- Respect and deal with similarities and differences in culture in families and society.
- Recognize the fact that some pupils have a different view of right and wrong to your own.
- In your class be clear with yourself about what is acceptable behaviour and what is not.

In your relationships with pupils:

- Expect high standards of behaviour and work from everyone.
- Work systematically with them towards a shared idea about what this means (ethos), e.g. through discussion as a class, in pairs and groups, to arrive at definition and examples of these in action.
- Recognize that being fair does not mean treating everyone exactly the same way.
- Being approachable does not mean that the children are your friends.
- Being firm means being just in your dealing and recognizing that not everyone starts from the same place.
- Rewards and punishments may not be the same for all children.

Development

The moral and social development of learners needs to inform the decisions you make about the values you teach and the ethos you establish with your classes. The aim is always to be stretching pupils' abilities to make the right choices. You'll want to develop a climate in which it is right to challenge the opinions of others, where acceptance of difference is normal and where ideas about social justice can be explored. This line of a strong but tolerant morality is not easy to establish. Your reputation with pupils for being fair has to be carefully built. Children expect you to be 'in charge' but they also expect you to respect and value their views and opinions, especially where these are at variance from accepted social norms.

Further reading

Haydon, G. (1997) *Teaching About Values: A New Approach*, London: Cassell.

Mosely, J. (1999) *More Quality Circle Time*, Cambridge: LDA.

Mosely, J. (1996) *Quality Circle Time*, Cambridge: LDA, both these are 'how to' books with many ideas about developing values and ethos.

Moyles, J. (1995) (Ed.) *Beginning Teaching: Beginning Learning in Primary Education*, Buckingham: Open University. Chapter 10 by Sylvia McNamarra 'Let's co-operate! Developing children's social skills in the classroom', is very useful.

TTA Standards

1.3, 3.3.1.

Whole class teaching

The Hay McBer Report (2000: 1.2.7) confirms that, 'what we saw effective teachers doing was a great deal of direct instruction to whole classes, interspersed with individual and small group work'. They comment on the high level of interaction between pupils and teacher. Whole class teaching has to involve all the children in the class. It is important that the work is differentiated; you have to engage all the children. A wide ability range may test the teacher's ability to do this. Recognize that some children take much longer to learn what others learn with ease. You'll want to have some tasks that everyone does, some that differentiate, and some to challenge the quick finishers. You'll want to make best use of any classroom assistants. None of this is achieved without high levels of planning and preparation.

Links

Whole class teaching may require thought about each of these:

Demonstration by the teacher
Differentiation
Discipline
Explaining
Group work
Independent learning
Instruction
Learning styles
Pace
Questioning
Timing within lessons
Transitions
Working with other adults

Strategies

In whole class teaching:

- Use a variety of teaching strategies.
- Teaching and learning activities must match learning outcomes.
- Use clear instructions, demonstrations, explanations and careful questioning.
- During the lesson find out what pupils know and understand.
- Use carefully chosen examples, case studies and other activities that allow pupils to explore their learning.
- Differentiate the work, for example, one approach is to have tasks that are different for the least and most able pupils and some that everyone does. It is important to meet the learning needs of each child in your class.

Development

Whole class teaching only works if the relationships between you and those you teach is interactive. The interactions between you and the children have to be based on respect and trust. Whole class teaching is at its best when learners are challenged to use higher order thinking. You'll want to use open ended questions,

188 Whole class teaching

asking pupils to explain their answers, relating your questions to their ability. You'll also want to keep your teaching fresh. For example, whilst for many of the whole class lessons you may follow a similar pattern, from time to time surprise the class with a different format.

It is worth recognizing that whilst whole class teaching is a popular method of teaching it is not universally regarded as successful. You'll note that effective teachers use individual and group work as well. You should read the entries on group work and on independent learning. Getting a balance of teaching and learning approaches that suits your class will be your aim.

Further reading

Banks, F. and Shelton Mayes, A. (Eds) (2001) *Early Professional Development for Teachers*, London: Open University/David Fulton. Section 2 has many articles about effective teaching.
McBer, H. (2000) *Research into Teacher Effectiveness: A Model of Teacher Effectiveness*, Department for Education and Employment weblink www.dfes.gov.uk/teachingreforms/leadership/mcber/
Moyles, J. (1995) (Ed.) *Beginning Teaching: Beginning Learning in Primary Education*, Buckingham: Open University.
Muijs, D. and Reynolds, D. (2001) *Effective Teaching: Evidence and Practice*, London: PCP.

TTA Standard

3.1.1.

Working with other adults

Time was when a teacher went into a classroom, closed the door and got on with teaching. These days you can expect to share the responsibility for children's progress with other adults, for at least some of the time. You'll regularly work with learning assistants (LA) and other classroom assistants (CA). If you work with children under 5 you'll work with nursery nurses (NN). You'll have contact with information technology technicians (ICT), lunchtime supervisors, janitors, cleaners, maintenance workers and school office staff. These are just some of your co-workers.

In the classroom, nursery nurses and learning and classroom assistants will expect you to know what it is you want them to do. They will also expect you to respect their expertise. Nursery nurses are trained and are often very experienced staff. Your learning and classroom assistants may also have considerable experience. It is becoming much more usual for all assistants to have opportunities to gain qualifications and for there to be a career structure for them as well. ICT technicians have mastery over the systems in the school. Often they know about suitable software and how to get children learning from ICT.

The nursery nurse, or classroom or learning assistant, should be your best ally. The relationship you have is going to be important to both of you. Often CAs are there to help you to work effectively with all the children by, for example, supporting the group of children for whom English is an additional language. The LA may be supporting a child with SEN. In early years classes, the NNs' expertise, for example, in setting up appropriate indoor and outdoor play, is something to be appreciated and encouraged. Your co-workers' relationships with children and parents are just as professional as yours, but because their position is different they often have a different understanding about the children from yours. Their views can add to your knowledge and inform the decisions you make. Some areas of your work are confidential; it is important to recognize that this can conflict with the open relationship you'll want to have with them.

Plan your teaching to make best use of the help available. Co-workers need to be involved all the time to make best use of teaching time. Beyond the nursery, in particular, think about what the assistant needs to do when you are teaching the whole class. What is their role when you are explaining something to the whole class or managing a question and answer session? This is something to consult them about.

Links

Teachers' employment and conditions
Teaching in teams

Strategies

Support co-workers by:

- Being clear about what you want them to do to support children's learning and your teaching:
    make sure you make good use of their time;
    both tell them about and write down the tasks to be done;

give them the materials for the tasks you set;
ask for feedback;
remember to say, 'thank-you' for the support they give.

- Including them in planning, in monitoring and assessing the children they work with.
- Agreeing on the class routines and procedures, making sure that you all discipline the children in similar ways.
- Involving them in problem solving and decision making. Together analyse, think about possible solutions, decide on actions and evaluate these.
- Recognizing and respecting their expertise and knowledge.
- Meeting their training needs (as far as you are able).
- Allowing the chance for them to work on their own initiative.

Development

Who else is in school? There are also support roles from other agencies, social workers, educational psychologists, specialist teachers, nurses, doctors, dentists, examination invigilators, school bus drivers, cooks, the police, the list goes on and on. Many schools have volunteer helpers, parents and people from the community, local firms and sports teams. All these people add an extra dimension to your work. In particular, you will want to work out how to make use of volunteers' time in a way that respects them. Give them tasks that are educationally important, for example, helping children master an aspect of writing using a computer or by listening to readers. They will need your knowledge about the children to undertake these tasks effectively.

Thomas (1989) identified the following areas as having the potential to create problems. Role ambiguity, 'who is the teacher?', may be a problem for some, including the children. Unintentionally obstructing each other or duplicating tasks is something to be avoided. Clear job specifications, ways of working and conflict resolution strategies, need to be in place to make best use of additional adults. The children need to know who does what. In the classroom think about the talents that all the additional adults have and how to use these to best advantage.

Further reading

Bradley, C., Roaf, C. and Benton, P. (2000) 'Working effectively with learning support assistants' in Benton, P. and O'Brien, T. (Eds) *Special Needs and the Beginning Teacher*, London: Continuum, pp. 171–91. The focus on special needs support is a useful introduction to thinking about how to work with all co-workers.

O'Brien, T. and Guiney, D. (2001) *Differentiation in Teaching and Learning, Principles and Practice*, London: Continuum.

Thody, A., Gray, B. and Bowden, D. (2000) *The Teacher's Survival Guide*, London: Continuum.

Thomas, G. (1989) 'The teacher and others in the classroom' in Cullingford, C. (Ed.) *The Primary Teacher: The Role of the Educator and the Purpose of Primary Education*, London: Cassell pp. 59–70.

TTA Standards

1.6, 3.1.4, 3.3.13.